# DAVENPORT'S CALIFORNIA WILLS AND ESTATE PLANNING LEGAL FORMS

# DAVENPORT'S CALIFORNIA WILLS AND ESTATE PLANNING LEGAL FORMS

## WITH 2024-2025 UPDATES

written by attorneys
**Alex Russell and Robert Maxwell**

SEE BOOKS AND LEGAL FORMS AT
**WWW.DAVENPORTPUBLISHING.COM**

## PUBLICATION DATA
(informal, library may use different data)

Names: Russell, Alex, 1972- author ;  Maxwell, Robert, 1960- author

Title: Davenport's California Wills And Estate Planning Legal Forms

Other Titles: Davenport's Wills

Description: Davenport Publishing 2023

Suggested Identifiers:  9798386492212, LCCN 2021909030, 9798748423373

Subjects: LCSH:      Wills--United States;
                            Wills--United States--Forms;
                            Estate Planning--United States;
                            Legal Forms

Classification:      LFF KF755 .C55 2022 (or as library chooses)
                            DDC 346.73 Rus--dc23 (or as library chooses)

9 8 7 6 5 4 3 2 1 0 0 0 0 0 2 3

## WARNING

**THIS PUBLICATION IS NOT A SUBSTITUTE FOR LEGAL ADVICE.** Publisher and authors say and warn this publication is not giving any legal, accounting, or other professional services or advice, which if wanted can be obtained by consulting in person an attorney or some other professional. **<u>No attorney-client relationship or any relationship creating a duty or obligation is agreed to or created by the purchase or use of this publication or forms</u>.**

# BOOKS AND FORMS FOR OTHER STATES ARE AVAILABLE.
SEE <u>WWW.DAVENPORTPUBLISHING.COM</u> FOR INFORMATION.

# CHAPTER 1
# BOOK BASICS AND LIST OF FORMS

## ESTATE PLANNING CONTROLS THINGS IF LATER ABSENT, SICK, OR DEAD

From Davenport Publishing and written by attorneys this book is on "Estate Planning", about doing legal documents to control health care, property, money, children, funeral, and more if later absent, sick, or dead. People have a legal right to control their health care, property, money, and family issues, and so judges, doctors, and others mostly just ask: **"Based on what a person wrote what did they likely want done?"**

## ESTATE PLANNING MOSTLY IS DOING SIMPLE THINGS IN 3 AREAS

Estate Planning is mostly doing simple things in 3 areas: After Death, Health Care, and Giving Power. Legal forms can make binding legal documents in these areas. **Many people use just 1 to 3 legal forms**.

---

### THERE ARE 9 LEGAL FORMS FOR CALIFORNIA IN THIS BOOK

#### AFTER DEATH FORMS

**Form 1. Will (Standard)** – a Will (also called "Last Will And Testament") lets person control things after their death like who gets their money and property, who is Executor, and allow helpful legal options later.

**Form 2. Will (Guardian)** – this Will has part added to name someone as Guardian to care for minor child under 18 if later needed (like if later no parent is available) and also manage child's money and property.

**Form 3. California Statutory Will** – the state legislature put this Will into statute law for people to find and use if they want, and it is a bit inflexible but is simple and well known by judges.

**Form 4. Handwritten Will** – this Will skips the usual need for 2 witnesses which saves time and work, but it must be all handwritten by the person doing the Will (so no use of typing, computers, or legal forms).

**Form 5. Tangible Personal Property List** – lets person easily outside a Will write more gifts to occur after death of "tangible personal property" like furniture, jewelry, vehicles, art, electronics, tools, and clothes.

#### HEALTH CARE FORMS

**Form 6. Advance Health Care Directive** – in case they're incapacitated later lets person name someone as "Agent" to control health care, give health care instructions, and maybe do serious step of saying <u>later</u> stop care if incapacitated and bad health likely won't improve (this part is often called doing a "Living Will") -- this form also can give Agent power over the dead body and funeral, burial, cremation, and related issues.

**Form 7. Physician Orders For Life-Sustaining Treatment** – does serious act of saying <u>immediately from now on</u> do not try certain health care listed (this is sometimes called the "Do Not Resuscitate" form).

#### GIVING POWER FORMS

**Form 8. Uniform Statutory Form Power Of Attorney** – lets power over money, property, and more be given to trusted person so they have legal power to do things, like use accounts, pay bills, and sell property.

**Form 9. Authorization To Consent To Medical Treatment Of A Minor** – lets a parent or guardian of child under age 18 give power to someone over child's health care to let them make decisions if needed.

## CALIFORNIA ESTATE PLANNING LAW APPLIES TO MOST PEOPLE HERE

This book is for California only. The law and legal documents can be <u>very</u> different in different states. <u>Whether local Estate Planning law applies is based on primary residence</u> of a person (their "domicile"). Judges often say residence occurs if people live in a place with no plans to leave in the indefinite future. Later plans to move changes nothing till people move. People <u>can</u> stay under a state's Estate Planning laws even if they leave and have no local home if it's temporary and people always keep firm plans to return. For example some people who leave months or more for travel, for school, for special work projects, and for the military may qualify to still be tied to their old state. Illegal immigrants can do Estate Planning. <u>For health care people often do legal documents to match the state a hospital or other facility is located in</u>.

## BOOK IS SHORT, HAS FORMS TO QUICKLY SEE, AND USES EMPHASIS

This book is short and may read rough but can be read quickly. Long books tend to lead to skimming and misunderstanding. The book has many legal forms people can quickly see. For emphasis paragraph titles, underlining, and boxes are used. This book capitalizes words like Will, Testator, and Agent but this is optional. To save space some small words are skipped and end quotation marks put before punctuation.

## LEGAL FORMS CAN HELP AND THIS BOOK PROVIDES "STANDARD FORMS"

Estate Planning research shows <u>a surprising 60% of people die without doing anything, 19% use a lawyer, and 21% use legal forms</u>. Legal forms are good at most things involved in Estate Planning and can make binding legal documents that judges, doctors, families, banks, and others legally must follow. Also, often a hospital, state agency, charity, or state legislature has made a form most people use and call the "standard form", and doctors, judges, and others may not like to follow different forms. This book <u>does</u> use a standard form in an area if it exists or provides a suitable form. Lawyers often write their own forms.

## THIS BOOK COVERS MAJOR IDEAS AND SHOULD SUIT MOST PEOPLE

This book covers the main U.S. legal ideas on Estate Planning and most major ways California law is a bit different. <u>The book covers what most people want to know but is kept short</u>, and longer books tend to lead to people skimming or misunderstanding. <u>Some people may want to do more research or see a lawyer</u>. This book and its forms can't cover every issue that matters to everyone but <u>should suit people without strange situations or wishes</u> about Estate Planning, which is probably most people (like maybe over 90%). Strange situations or wishes that may need more research or a lawyer include: a) unusual wishes for gifts, b) wealth over $3 million, c) big medical concerns in family, d) property or money going to a person with disability or special needs, and e) wish to hide or move assets to quickly qualify for government programs.

## ESTATE PLANNING OFTEN IS NOT THAT IMPORTANT

Estate Planning is often not vital and worth much time or money, and may not affect costs, delays, work, and other things as much as claimed. For young adults and parents the benefits seem very low since only about 9% of people die by 60, and only about 0.13% of children under 18 had 2 parents die to need help. *Social Security Tables: Felicitie Bell*; *Census Life Factors Mortality Study #288*. A lawyer can be used for Estate Planning but they can cost $1000s, take months of work, and make mistakes. In life people weigh costs, benefits, and risks and often go with a low cost option. If people really want to help family they can buy life insurance ($100,000 of term life by just questionnaire ("simplified issue") is about $500/year.

# CHAPTER 2
# TERMS, PROPERTY, AND HELPFUL INFORMATION FORM

## THERE ARE BASIC TERMS AND IDEAS IN ESTATE PLANNING

Some legal terms and ideas are basic to Estate Planning.

■ "Estate Planning" is a person doing legal documents to control things if later absent, sick, or dead. After a document is signed people are usually still free to sell or transfer property, instruct doctors, or change forms.

■ A "person doing a legal document" and "doing a form" means the form is for and affects that person.

■ A "Will" or "will" (this book uses upper case "W") is a legal document done to control issues after death. The phrase "Last Will And Testament" is used since a "Testament" long ago was a small document done along with a Will to do some things. If no Will is done a person is described as being "intestate".

■ A person who died is called "decedent" or the "deceased". A person getting a Will gift is called "recipient", "beneficiary", or "heir" if related (they "inherit"). "Survive" or "surviving" is to be alive after someone died.

■ Someone picked by a person to do things after their death is called by most people the "Executor".

■ A person doing a Will is called "Testator" or "Will maker". Before about 1990 a woman Testator was called a "Testatrix" and woman Executor called an "Executrix" but this is no longer often done.

■ "Probate" is a legal process to do things after death like transfer property, authorize a Guardian, and handle creditors. Due to nice changes in law probate is now often "informal", faster, and less expensive.

■ The "estate" is both a) all property and money of person that at their death did not automatically transfer to other owners, and b) the entity run by an Executor several months to hold items and do things (sort of like a small corporation). For example accounts may be renamed, like: "Estate of John Smith (deceased)".

■ Property is: 1) "real property" (land and buildings), 2) "fixtures" (things tied to real property like fences and wired-in appliances), or 3) "personal property" (everything else like clothes, cars, cash, and investments).

■ Legal documents to control health care things are often called "Advanced Directives", but names vary.

■ In California a person under 18 is called a "minor" and a parent or "Guardian" mostly handles their affairs. A minor or other person not reasonably able to make wise decisions lacks "capacity" and is "incapacitated".

■ Forms giving power to someone are often called "Power of Attorney" forms. The person giving power is called the "Principal" and person getting power is called the "Attorney-in-Fact" or "Agent".

■ State law is called the "California Statutes" which is grouped in a few dozen "Codes". Estate Planning is mostly handled in the "Probate Code". A single law is called a section or statute often shown by "s" or "§". For example one law is: "Cal. Prob. Code § 6132". A form found in state law is called a "statutory form".

## LEGAL DOCUMENTS MAY NEED TO BE "WITNESSED" OR "NOTARIZED"

Legal documents to be valid may need to be "witnessed", which is someone acting as witness watching person doing form sign and then witness signs. Documents may need to be "notarized", which is person who is a "notary" (also called "notary public") see signing and use ink stamp on page and then notary signs too. Notaries are found at some banks, brokers, insurance agents, courts, and government offices but they are often busy or just help current customers. A helpful notary often can be found using a phonebook and calling.

## ANYONE CAN FILL IN MOST OF A FORM, AND LATER TRY TO KEEP ORIGINAL

When filling out a form except for certain special forms and except for signatures other parts can be filled in by a person not doing the form for themselves. After a legal form is completed and signed usually people try to keep the original and hand out copies but situations vary. Some people do "multiple originals" by having everyone sign identical documents to have many pages with real ink signatures, but this can be confusing.

## PROBABLY DO NEW FORMS IF DIVORCE, MARRY, HAVE CHILD, OR MOVE

Divorcing, marrying, birth or adoption of child, or moving to a new state can have major legal effects. If any of these events occur it is recommended people do a new Will and other Estate Planning papers soon. To help most states say a Will from another state is still valid but this is not always certain.

## "INTESTATE" LAW SAYS WHERE THINGS GO AT DEATH IF THERE IS NO WILL

State "intestate law" says where a dead person's property and money goes if no valid Will was done (except for certain rights of spouses, family, and creditors). This often says half and sometimes all goes (in order) to any spouse, half or any remainder to decedent's children natural or adopted, then next close family, and then the state. Some people are happy with how intestate law would transfer things and skip a Will.

---

### NO FEDERAL OR CALIFORNIA TAX IS USUALLY OWED AT A DEATH

Usually no tax is owed as a result of a death, including no estate, inheritance, death, or similar taxes. This is since the "Federal Estate And Gift Tax" only starts when tax credit is used up covering $13.99 million per person in 2025 and later. California no longer has any inheritance, estate, or similar taxes.

---

## PERSON CAN ONLY GIFT IN WILL WHAT THEY OWN AT DEATH

A person can only gift by Will things they own at death, so people should research what they own.

## OWNERSHIP CAN BE SIMPLE, BUT MARRIED PEOPLE FACE SPECIAL ISSUES

Often what a person owns is simple. Property law says a person usually owns all they earn as wages and salary, their share of income and profit tied to property they own, and owns or partly owns any things their money or property buys or improves. For items with "title" documents (real estate or vehicles) or where there is a "listed owner" (like accounts) the named persons are often legal owners unless evidence shows special facts. A person during life can sell property, make gifts, or transfer things even if they are named in a Will, so people should consider if they already sold or gave away property they name in a Will gift. And as this book says later, for married people "Community Property Law" often splits ownership of money and property 50/50 between spouses, so married people may face issues in gifting by Will or other ways.

## THINGS OWNED IN SPECIAL WAYS MAY LIMIT GIFTING IN WILL

A person should consider if they own real estate or other property in special ways which may limit gifting by Will. Laws in different states vary but some special joint ways are:

a) "joint tenant with right of survivorship" or similar legal options, so then property transfers automatically to the other named owners regardless of a Will, which in some states is usually how the family house is held,

b) papers say a "life estate" exists, so then if life of someone ends the other people in papers get item, and

c) "Trust property" will be transferred as paperwork says, if paperwork made a Trust entity and property was transferred into it, so then the Trust papers tell a Trustee where to transfer things at person's death.

Normal joint property for the part owned <u>can</u> be gifted by Will, like "I give my half of boat to Paul Lucas Fox". Joint ownership can come from joint papers, agreement, use of joint funds, or a gift was to multiple persons.

---

## WARNING: "NON-PROBATE PROPERTY" TRANSFERS IGNORE ANY WILL

Money or property that for some reason automatically transfers on death or soon after to new owners is called "non-probate property". Examples of non-probate property are: a) if a "designated beneficiary" form was done to name persons to get account or investment, b) transfer-on-death account, and c) real estate like a house held by 2 people as "joint tenants with survivorship" or similar so survivor gets things. Insurance with a beneficiary usually ignores a Will. <u>Trying to do non-probate transfers for all things is called "avoiding probate"</u>, but it is rare as it may make living and paperwork a hassle for years, benefits are small, and it is hard to not miss an item and fail. <u>People should consider non-probate transfers that will occur automatically on death and consider what property and money will be left to transfer by Will.</u>

---

## SOME LESS COMMON AND LESS USEFUL FORMS ARE NOT IN THIS BOOK

This book skips less common or less useful documents.

1. A "Codicil" can modify a Will but it is easier and safer to just re-do a Will.

2. As explained later California does <u>not</u> usually use an "affidavit" done with a notary to support a Will.

3. Some people do a "Revocable Living Trust" so Trust entity with Trustee holds property or money during their life however long, usually done to after death avoid small delay, costs, or work (by "avoiding probate"). This is rare as it requires immediately moving most of a person's things into a Trust causing maybe years of hassles, mostly for small benefits for people who are probably happy to later do work to get things by Will.

4. "Childrens Trust" papers can be done so Trust upon a death gets a minor child's money or property to manage until 18, but this is uncommon due to possible years of hassle and costs and (as this book shows) since it rarely matters and most Wills already arrange Guardian and other people to help a child if needed.

5. Some people do a "Pet Trust" to help a pet, but it's easier to just give money in Will to person given a pet.

6. Separate forms can be done but <u>most people handle any organ donation in drivers license or state ID forms</u>.

7. Complex documents may be suggested for tax reasons but as this book explains taxes are rarely an issue.

## SOME PEOPLE DO "HELPFUL INFORMATION" FORM FOR FRIENDS AND FAMILY

It is <u>not a real legal form that legally does anything but a person can do a "Helpful Information" form</u> so family or friends after a death <u>have more information</u> about property, money, debts, documents, and more. Often a person does the form quickly and attaches printed pages to show what is owned. <u>See next pages</u>.

# ESTATE PLANNING HELPFUL INFORMATION

For more space attach copies of form or blank pages.  Keep pages by a Will or other place for Executor or family.

1. Personal Information (Name, Birthdate, Social Security number, special family details, other):

2. Real estate, vehicles, and other major tangible property (especially if people may not find them):

3. Non-tangible assets like stocks, accounts, investments, loans owed you, and business interests:

4. Possible income or insurance like pensions, retirement, disability, insurance, or contracts:

5. Debts owed by you like credit card, loan, student loan, mortgage, car loans, and accounts payable:

6. Names and information of professionals used (attorneys, accountants, brokers, doctors, others):

7. Computer passwords and helpful files, document places, and safes or safe-deposit boxes code/key:

8. Other helpful things, wishes for funeral, special requests, and last messages to family and friends:

# CHAPTER 3
# WILL BASICS

## WILL LETS "TESTATOR" CONTROL SOME THINGS AFTER DEATH

A Will is done by a person to control some things after their death. A person doing a Will is called the "Testator" or "Will maker". A Testator <u>when signing</u> must be at least 18 years old, of sound mind (rational with sufficient memory), and not be under duress (unfair pressure or threat). Most people can do a Will.

## CANCELING OLD WILLS IS USUALLY NOT A PROBLEM

So a new Will is followed old Wills should be canceled ("revoked") but this is easy and rarely a problem. <u>A new Will often says old Wills are revoked to cancel them, and all the Will forms in this book start with this</u>. Also to revoke a Will a person can write "void" or "cancelled" or "X" on a Will, preferably with a witness to this. Usually crossing out just part of a Will has no effect, and revoking a Will doesn't bring back an earlier Will.

## USUALLY SIGN WILL IN FRONT OF 2 WITNESSES WHO THEN SIGN

## USUALLY A WILL TO BE VALID MUST BE WRITTEN AND HAVE 2 WITNESSES

Usually to be a valid California Will it must a) show it is meant as a Will, b) be written, and c) be signed in front of 2 witnesses who sign too. A Will must be put on paper and a "Video Will", "Audio Will", or online or computer Will is powerless. Verbal promises about things after death are mostly invalid if not in a Will. California law says witnesses signing is enough to use a Will later, and <u>no notary or affidavit is needed</u> unlike many states. <u>As this book later explains California does lets a Will skip the 2 witnesses if it's all handwritten</u>.

## WITNESSES MUST BE AT LEAST 18 AND USUALLY NOT GETTING WILL GIFTS

<u>A person to act as witness must be at least age 18</u>. It is not required but preferable a witness not be old or live far away. A person who is named in a Will gift <u>can</u> witness the Will. But Will gifts to a witness are limited by law to what they'd get if there were no Will under intestate law unless they can prove there was no duress, menace, fraud, or undue influence. To avoid this problem many people try to use "disinterested" witnesses who are not named in Will gifts. Though not required most people also try to not use a witness named in Will as Executor or as Guardian. Often used as a Will witness is a friend, stranger, or family.

## TESTATOR AND 2 WITNESSES SIGN A WILL WHEN ALL TOGETHER

To complete a Will a Testator signs and then 2 witnesses sign usually within a few minutes. Everyone should be in 1 room and see each person sign. Witnesses usually quietly read the 1 paragraph they sign. Testator need not initial Will pages. Witnesses and Testator showing each other an ID is not required but is common. Testator or witness need not use their full legal name if they dislike it and rarely used it.

## WITNESSES MUST KNOW IT IS A WILL USUALLY BY TESTATOR TELLING THEM

In California the Will witnesses must know it is Testator's Will for it to be valid, and anyone can tell them of this but often the person doing a Will says it. This is often called "Testator publishing the Will" by lawyers. Often a Testator tells the 2 witnesses something like, "My name is _____ and this is the Will I want and do voluntarily and want you 2 people to witness". Some Testators also chat with witnesses a few minutes and mention the Will more to show they know what they're doing.

## KEEP SIGNED WILL IN SAFE PLACE IT CAN BE FOUND AFTER A DEATH

Once done people should keep Will so it can be found within days of a death, like in desk, drawer, safe, or less often a safe deposit box. It can be given to a person to hold. It may help to tell people where to find a Will and any needed code or keys. In California a Will can't be filed at court until the person who did Will is dead.

## MOST WILLS SAY USE LESS COSTLY AND SHORTER "INFORMAL" PROBATE

To help most Wills authorize "informal probate" which is a legal option to reduce some costs and delays. Usually probate after a death is not too costly or slow, and often over 95% of value gets to wanted persons.

## MOST WILLS SAY TO SKIP COSTLY BOND

Most Wills say no "bond" or "surety" is needed for Executor, Guardian, or similar. Most people do not want a bond since it is insurance against misconduct paid with estate money and they trust people they named.

## JOINT WILL SIGNED BY BOTH SPOUSE IS NOT RECOMMENDED

A "Joint Will" or "Contract To Make A Will" which a lawyer can write can bind a married couple to gift everything to other at death and then to their children, but this is rare, has issues, and banned some places.

---

### WILL NAMES AN EXECUTOR TO DO THINGS AFTER A DEATH

## CAN NAME PERSON "EXECUTOR" TO HAVE POWER TO ACT AFTER A DEATH

Most people in their Will name someone as "Executor" to do things after their death. The law gives an Executor power to act, like transfer property and money to new owners, handle creditors, and do probate. If a Will does not name an Executor a judge can pick someone, but family may argue about who to pick. Often named Executor is a spouse, adult child, other family, or friend. A lawyer or bank can be Executor if they are paid a large fee. Naming 2 people to both do the job is possible but rare due to risk of arguments and delay, and since any 1 person named is usually trusted. The person named Executor can get Will gifts. In California most people use the term Executor for this but some use "Personal Representative" or, also, "Administrator" if a judge picked the person. A lawyer or bank can be Executor but they charge high fees.

## EXECUTOR OFTEN GETS LIMITED PAY AND ESTATE PAYS FOR OTHER THINGS

California has a fee schedule for Executors and Attorneys which suggests paying them each a fairly high 4% of most assets handled without deductions for mortgages or liens. Some people think this is too much. Due to this many Wills say Executor will be paid a fixed amount and not the standard fee, and this book's Will forms say Executor will be paid $900. Executors often just skip asking for pay to avoid income tax and leave more in the estate to do Will gifts. Other money an Executor or estate needs for things like repairs, insurance, costs, fees, lawyer, and utilities is usually gotten from estate accounts or selling property.

## EXECUTOR IS PERSON AT LEAST 18, AND SECOND PERSON RARELY NEEDED

A person to be Executor must be 18 or older. They needn't be a state resident or even U.S. citizen but being local makes their later work easier. A judge later may not let someone they think is unsuitable serve as Executor especially if it involves past crimes. A judge can remove a person doing a bad job as Executor. Some people name a 2nd person to serve if 1st person is unavailable, but most skip this since it's rarely needed, if a problem is seen a new Will can be done, or a judge can pick someone. To add a 2nd person for this words can be added to a Will, like: "or if they are reasonably unable to serve I name _____ to serve".

# CHAPTER 4
# WILL GIFTS INCLUDING RESIDUE

## MAIN USE OF WILL IS TO SAY GIFTS TO HAPPEN AFTER DEATH

People use a Will mostly to say what happens to their property and money after their death, usually by making various Will gifts. Verbal and even most written statements about this are not usually valid if outside a Will. A Will can control property acquired after it was signed. Note, after a death some families if all agree may informally hand out small items in ways a decedent mentioned they wanted, but this is not fully proper.

## GIFTING IN WILL USING SIMPLE WORDS OFTEN IS BEST

Making gifts in a Will using simple words is often best, using words like "I give to" and "I gift to". This is legally fine and avoids confusing legal words like "bequest", "devise", and "legacy" which few people know.

## PEOPLE ARE MOSTLY FREE TO GIFT THEIR THINGS AS WANTED

People are mostly free to give at death their money and property as they want, like give a child nothing, give all to a charity, or give all to a friend. But family may have some rights which this book covers later.

## IN WILL CAN DO "SPECIFIC GIFTS" TO GIFT PARTICULAR PROPERTY

Most Wills have "specific gifts" to gift underline particular things. Specific gifts can be any property, like "I give boat to Ed Blom" and "I give UBank account #84553873 to Sue Wu". If a gift is not clear the law assumes all of a kind of thing is given, like "I give jewelry to Ann Po" means all jewelry. But gifting specific property can have surprises like value of an item can change, or a Will gift may fail to occur later if property is no longer owned.

## IN WILL CAN DO "GENERAL GIFTS" LIKE OF MONEY

Wills can do "general gifts" where what is gifted is not particular property but can be flexibly chosen, like "I give 1 of my 3 cars to Ed Po" which lets an Executor pick which car. The usual general gift is money, like "I give $5 to Ed Vu". Money gifts are easy to write, let equal gifts be made, and are safer since specific items might not be owned at death. To carry out money gifts an Executor uses accounts or sells some property.

## "RESIDUE CLAUSE" IS CATCH-ALL THAT HELPFULLY GIFTS ANYTHING LEFT

Most Wills by their end have a Residue Clause to gift property or money not gifted or used in Will or other way, sometimes called a "catch-all" or "left-over" clause. The Residue Clause is covered later in this Chapter.

## CALIFORNIA LAW LETS "GIFT LISTS" BE USED TO GIFT CERTAIN PROPERTY

This book later shows how California law lets "Gift Lists" gift tangible personal property outside of a Will.

## PERSON IN WILL GIFT USUALLY MUST SURVIVE OR GIFT DOES NOT OCCUR

Many Wills like this book's Will forms say person named in Will gift must survive (live past) Testator for the gift to occur unless gift language specifically says different. If survival is not clearly required for a Will gift what then occurs if a named recipient is dead can be unclear (like due to confusing state "anti-lapse" laws). People doing a Will should consider how Will gifts to people dying before Testator usually have no effect. Many people if they see person in a Will gift has died re-do Will or just trust the Residue Clause to handle it.

## SOME PEOPLE ADD "ALTERNATE BENEFICIARY" MAYBE FOR SPECIAL ITEMS

A person named in a Will gift dying before a Testator is rare, and if seen most people just re-do Will to add new person or let Will's Residue Clause handle it. Some people to prepare for this chance maybe for special items write in a gift an alternate beneficiary, like "I give boat to Ed Wu but if they don't survive me to Ann Wu".

---

## WILL CAN SAY IF RECIPIENT DIES A GIFT GOES TO "LINEAL DESCENDANTS"

A Will gift can say it goes to person but if they don't survive then to their "lineal descendants per stirpes". Descendants are a person's children and grandchildren. "Per stirpes" is about "how" to spread things and means "by root" or "by branch", and basically tries to divide things so each family branch gets equal share. A family branch that died off with no one left is ignored. Most Wills use "lineal descendants" language in a Residue Clause and it also can be put in other gifts if wanted. An example shows how it works:

A Will may say: **"Furniture to Sue Wu but if they don't survive to their lineal descendants per stirpes"**, and this means if Sue Wu died and her son Ken Wu is living and her other son Ben Wu has died but left 2 children then, legally, under the law Ken Wu himself gets 50% and Ben Wu's 2 children each get 25%.

---

## PROPERTY OR MONEY IN A "JOINT GIFT" GOES TO MULTIPLE PEOPLE

The same property or money in a "joint gift" can go to multiple people to each get a part interest, like "I give boat and all hats to Ann Wu and Sue Han" means each person owns 50% of every item. People later can split things by agreement or as Executor suggests, or Executor can sell items and split the money. If a person in a joint gift has died their part of things usually is left to transfer under a Residue Clause.

## GIFT BENEFICIARIES CAN GET PERCENTAGE RATHER THAN EQUAL SHARE

If a Will gift goes to multiple people the law assumes equal shares, but if wanted percentages can be put to make unequal gifts, like "I give boat 90% to Ed Wu and 10% to Joe Hud".

## CONDITIONS ON WILL GIFTS ARE RARE DUE TO POSSIBLE PROBLEMS

Putting conditions on a gift, like "I give Ann Poe $90 if she graduates college", can cause problems like years of delay, risk of lawsuits, and big attorneys fees, and due to this conditions are rarely put on Will gifts.

## HELPFUL LAWS OFTEN REQUIRE PERSON SURVIVE 120 HOURS TO GET GIFT

Laws in most states say a person dying within 120 hours of someone is seen as having died earlier. This avoids legal problems like need to know exact time of death if people die near each other, and often means a gift doesn't occur and avoids item going to someone who quickly dies so item must be transferred again.

## LATER DIVORCE OR MURDER CANCELS WILL GIFTS

California law says a person divorcing or murdering Testator usually cancels all Will gifts to the person.

## CAN LEAVE SOME WILL GIFT LINES BLANK OR WRITE THINGS LIKE "SKIPPED"

A person writing a Will can choose to not use some gifts lines in a Will legal form, like by just leaving them blank, writing things like "SKIPPED" or "NONE" in them, or using a computer to delete some gift lines. Judges and others usually do not care about neatness or empty spaces in Wills.

14

## RESIDUE CLAUSE GIFTING ALL LEFT IS MAIN WAY USED TO GIFT THINGS

## THE "RESIDUE CLAUSE" IS CATCH-ALL THAT HELPS GIFT ANYTHING LEFT

Most Wills by their end have a Residue Clause to gift any property or money not gifted earlier in Will or used in other ways. Things transferred this way is called the "Residue". Many people gift most their things this way by intentionally not mentioning in Will most property and money so it's handled by a Residue Clause. This skips need to describe things and has less legal risk. Later after a death after applying a Residue Clause if anything is left (which is rare) then closest heirs get things (this is closest family).

## USUAL RESIDUE CLAUSE HAS 2 PARTS

A short 2 part Residue Clause is usual and is used in this book's Wills, and it has:

1) 1st space to name 1 or more persons to get things if they survive Testator (many name a spouse or closest family here), and if several people are named but only some survive then survivors split things, and

2) 2nd space to name persons to get things if all in 1st space don't survive (so these are fallbacks) (many name next family or friends here), and if a person in 2nd space died their descendants get their share.

## EXAMPLE OF 2 PART RESIDUE CLAUSE:

"RESIDUE CLAUSE: I give money and property not gifted earlier:

A) to _____ my husband John Paul Doe _____ if they survive me, then

B) to _____ Sam Doe my son, Beth Wu my daughter, and Greta Fisher my friend _____ and if any of those just named do not survive me their part goes to their lineal descendants, per stirpes."

In this example if John Paul Doe has survived then he gets all things, but if John Paul Doe hasn't survived and also Sam Doe hasn't survived and he left 2 daughters then those 2 daughters split the 1/3 share of Sam Doe so get 1/6 each and other 2 persons in second part Beth Wu and Greta Fisher get 1/3 each.

## A FEW PEOPLE RE-WRITE A RESIDUE CLAUSE TO HAVE 1 PART

A normal Residue Clause of 2 parts is often fine and basically person put in 1st part usually gets things. A small fraction of people may want to modify a Will to have a "1 Part Residue Clause" which gifts to a group more equally. People with no spouse and no children are likelier to do this change, but even they often don't bother and just use this book's Will forms as is. See Example below for exact words to use if people want this change to a 1 Part Residue Clause.

## EXAMPLE OF 1 PART RESIDUE CLAUSE:

"RESIDUE CLAUSE: The rest, residue, and remainder of my estate, property of any kind and nature, and anything I have an interest in, I give to _ Adam Doe and Beth Wu _ who survive me, and to lineal descendants per stirpes of any person just named who did not survive me."

In this example if Adam hasn't survived but had 2 children they each get 25%, and if Beth Wu survived she gets 50%. Or if Beth Wu also hadn't survived and had 5 kids they split her part and each gets 10%.

## MUST SUFFICIENTLY DESCRIBE NAMES AND PROPERTY IN WILL GIFTS

### WILL GIFT IS FINE IF PEOPLE CAN TELL WHAT TESTATOR LIKELY MEANT

The basic legal rule is a <u>Will gift is sufficiently detailed if people who knew Testator can inform Executor or a judge what Testator meant more likely than not</u>, and certainty is not needed to carry out a Will gift.

### PUTTING NAMES OF PEOPLE OR GROUPS IN WILL GIFTS IS FAIRLY EASY

Names in Wills are fairly easy. It is assumed people gift to people they know so it's OK to use common names unless 2 friends or family have same name. Details can be added if names may not be recognized or to be friendly, like "I give $5 to waitress in town Ann Ax" and "I give $5 to my loyal funny friend Ed Grant". If people used a nickname "also known as" or "a/k/a" may help, like "I give $5 to Ed Wu a/k/a Old Fishy". Gifts can go to non-persons like a government, charity, or group if they're a real organization. Examples are: "I give $5 to The Salvation Army, "I give $5 to Fresno City Library", "I give $50 to Ivy School, Hilo, Hawaii", and "I give all clothes to Bethel Church in Irvine, CA". People often phone to ask for full name of a charity.

### DESCRIPTIONS OF ITEMS IN WILL GIFTS IS FAIRLY EASY

Describing items in Wills is fairly easy since people rarely own similar items, so fine is "I give ax to Ed Wu" and "I give big table to Don Ho". It's OK to gift by list or category, like "I give cow, van, and TV to Ann Vix" or "I give tools to Ed Hill". Financial assets can use plain words, like "bank accounts" or "stocks", but some details can help, like "UBank account ending #2511". <u>Using item location in a Will gift is risky</u> as judges may ignore Will gifts if it seems items were placed to affect gifting and not "independently significant" life reason. So, "I give Ed Po items in safe and desk" a judge may not follow, but "I give Ed Po hats at cabin" likely is OK.

### DESCRIBING REAL PROPERTY IS HARD SO MANY USE RESIDUE OR TITLE

To give real property (real estate) in a Will <u>using a "legal description" is legally best</u> but is hard to do right. This can be paragraphs long, for example like: "Lot 3, Block 21 of Mann's Subdivision, Map Book 3, page 17, Records of Orange County, CA", or "Commence at NE Corner of the East ½ of West ½ of NE ¼ of SW ¼ of Section 17, Township 1 North, Range 12 West and then run South [...] and return to point of beginning". It is legally less safe <u>but common to gift real property with plain words</u>, like house by "I give 21 Ivy Rd., Napa, CA to Ian Leo Ax", or land like "I give all real property in Pine County, CA to Sue Ann Hu". A street address and legal description are often both used. Will gifts using a location give <u>all</u> real property and fixtures there.

<u>But the legally safest way to gift real property is 1) do nothing specific so it's covered by Will Residue Clause which covers things not specifically gifted other ways, or 2) have broker or lawyer add names to the land title.</u>

### SIMPLE WILL WITH MOST GIFTING DONE BY RESIDUE CLAUSE IS OFTEN BEST

Writing a simple Will without many gifts and much left blank and then using Residue Clause is often best.

If there <u>is a spouse</u> often people do a few small gifts to friends and other family, then use Residue Clause of Will to gift their spouse the Residue, and then name a few fallback persons in the Residue Clause.

If there is <u>no spouse and no child</u> often people do a few small gifts, then gift family or friends the Residue.

<u>A parent with young children</u> if married to other parent often gifts Residue to spouse, and as fallback gifts the Residue to the children. Or if not married a parent mostly gifts to their children using the Residue Clause.

# CHAPTER 5
# DEBT, MARRIAGE, AND YOUNG CHILD ISSUES

## DEBT, MARRIAGE, AND YOUNG CHILD CAN CAUSE ISSUES
This Chapter deals with debt, marriage, and young child. People can skip the parts they want to.

## DEBT ISSUES

## PAYING DECEDENT'S DEBTS MAY USE UP RESOURCES AND REDUCE GIFTS
Creditors a decedent owed can ask a judge to be paid from decedent's money and property before any Will gifts and other transfers are done, and how this occurs is set by law and a Will can skip saying this. Helpfully, for reasons shown in this book often creditors don't bother to act if family ignore them and say decedent left little of value, like under $50,000 and family house. Paying debts uses decedent's property and estate so may affect (in order) Will Residue, Will general gifts, Will specific gifts, and non-probate transfers. Some special things like probate fees, funeral, health care, and probate lawyer have priority to be paid first. People should consider how paying debts may use up money or property, leaving less to carry out Will gifts. Decedent's spouse or family aren't personally liable for decedent's debts unless they guaranteed or co-signed.

## BEFORE DEBTS ARE PAID MAY COME SOME CALIFORNIA FAMILY RIGHTS
Some state "family rights" can be claimed by a spouse or minor children under 18 before debts are paid. First, the "living allowance" right gives family from estate enough to live on for 1-2 years, often $4,000/month. Second, family can keep during probate most of decedent's personal property like stuff in the house, and later family often try to claim small items are "exempt from creditors" (or hide items from creditors or Executor). Third, the "small estate set-aside" probate option lets a spouse or minor child claim for themselves all in the estate if it's worth under $95,325 not counting the house, and this may mean a Will is not followed at all. Due to all this most people give most things to a spouse or minor children (like over 90% and family home) to avoid them wanting to use family rights which may interfere with Will gifts. People can research their state.

## CALIFORNIA "HOMESTEAD LAW" OFTEN PROTECTS HOME FOR FAMILY
State "homestead law" says, first, a person's house after death can't be bothered by creditors with no proper mortgage, home equity loan, mechanics lien, or similar (usually if married 2 spouses must sign these). Second, it says decedent's family can have possession of a family home owned by decedent (even if it was separate property) till spouse's death or children are 18. During this time they must pay mortgage, taxes, and insurance, and later the house goes to who a Will, title, or other thing says. Abandonment or present occupier and future owner agreeing to a sale can change this. Due to all this and to avoid delay and uncertainty most people give their house to a spouse or if no spouse to minor children by Will or putting them on the land title.

## OFTEN SECURED DEBTS LIKE MORTGAGE OR VEHICLE LIEN AREN'T PAID OFF
By law secured debts like house mortgage or vehicle lien are not usually paid off even if a Will says to pay debts. This avoids using up estate resources so there is enough to carry out more Will gifts. A Testator who want to help with a mortgage or lien can a) in Will give enough cash to pay off a mortgage or lien, or b) write an order to pay in a Will (like, "I order cabin mortgage paid off"). This book's Will forms say don't pay secured debts unless Testator writes to do so. If later not paid monthly any mortgages and liens can be foreclosed.

## "COMMUNITY PROPERTY" LAW APPLIES TO MARRIED PEOPLE IN CALIFORNIA

Nine states mostly in West U.S. for married people use "Community Property" law, and these states are California, Arizona, Louisiana, Idaho, Nevada, New Mexico, Texas, Washington, and Wisconsin. The other states use "Separate Property" law for married people (but it can be complicated if people recently moved). A very few people sign a contract about Community Property usually before a wedding. The law is complex.

## MARRIED SPOUSES MAY OWN MOST THINGS 50/50 EVEN WAGES AND SALARY

Community Property law says state residents if married share 50/50 and have a half-interest in money and property either spouse gets which is related in any way to physical or mental effort while married.

Shared things are called "community property" and all else is called "separate property". This law is from Spanish and other traditions, seeing marriage like a partnership, and so if a person's spouse dies the person has something to live on. Many states have laws to give any spouse a lot (often called "elective share" laws).

Wages, salary, and income related to a spouse's labor are community property no matter what spouses wish.

## SHOWING THINGS ARE NOT COMMUNITY PROPERTY CAN BE HARD

A judge will accept what spouse and family say is Community Property, but if it's disputed the law presumes a married person's things are community property till proven otherwise. Good records, separate accounts, or discussing ownership with witnesses can help **but is rarely done**. Putting 1 name on an account or title to a thing doesn't change its nature. Many couples end up with **most** property and money as community property.

Examples of separate property are an inheritance or gift given to 1 spouse, personal injury lawsuit money, engagement and wedding rings, and anything owned before marriage including savings and any property.

Separate property can come from tracing things to other separate property, like if pre-marriage money pays half a car's price it can be half separate property, if pre-marriage money pays to fix up property the increase in value can be separate property, and if pre-marriage property is sold for cash the cash is separate property.

A spouse spending effort on separate property can make it be all or partly community property, like personally doing big repairs or remodeling, actively managing a business, or actively trading stocks or a collection.

## MARRIED PEOPLE FACE ISSUES AND HAVE SOME OPTIONS WHEN GIFTING

Married people face some issues with gifting by Will and other ways things, including as this book has said due to community property, family rights, and homestead rights. Married people have some options.

**First, to avoid issues many people just give everything wholly to their spouse by Will or other ways.**

Second, some people are careful to only gift separate property to persons not their spouse by Will and other ways, and then have all community property go to a spouse. But this can be hard to do with certainty.

Third, some people trust if they give most money and property to their spouse (like over 90% and the family home) the spouse won't object to a small fraction of community property going to other people, and instead will cooperate with Executor in all ways. A spouse often doesn't want the hassle, to appear selfish, or risk a lawsuit that may come just to keep a half-interest in bit of community property a decedent gave to someone.

# YOUNG CHILD ISSUES

## WILL CAN NAME "GUARDIAN" TO CARE FOR CHILD AND THEIR PROPERTY

If a parent dies with child under age 18 the other natural or adopted parent (but not step-parent) instantly gets control of their care including health care, school, and home issues, unless the parent is proven unfit in court which is rare. In case it is needed (like if both parents are dead) a Will often names a "Guardian of the Person" to provide this care for child, and often named is a healthy and willing family member or friend.

Since a child until 18 can't easily manage money or property many Wills name a "Guardian of the Estate" for any young child to manage their property and money, and say how to use these for a child's costs like living costs, school, and health care till usually 18 when all left goes to child. People paying things for child can ask to be paid from a child's money and property. A judge often holds an annual hearing about this. Note, if a person needs help managing their finances after age 18 usually the term "Conservator" is used.

This book's Will forms have a spot to name people to be **both** Guardian of the Person and also Guardian of the Estate. Not bothering to name different people for this is common since parents dying is rare, a child often gets property and money only if both parents are dead so a Guardian will be involved, people chosen as wise enough to raise children usually are at least OK with finances, and a Guardian if they don't get all power may argue or sue for spending. People who want can modify a Will to name different people for this.

## GUARDIAN MUST BE 18 OR OLDER AND ALTERNATE RARELY IS NEEDED

A person must be at least 18 to be a Guardian. They need not be a state resident or even U.S. citizen but being local makes their work easier. Preference of last living parent gets more weight. A judge later may block a person who seems unsuited. The same 1 person can be named Executor, Guardian, and other positions to keep things simple. If no Will names a Guardian or they're unavailable a judge can pick person, but family may argue about this. Naming 2 people to help a child to act at the same time is rarely done since the 2 may argue and any 1 person named is trusted, but some people name a stable married couple. Some Wills add a 2nd person in case 1st person is unavailable, but many people skip this since it is rarely needed, if a problem is seen a Will can be re-done, and a judge always can act. If wanted, to add a 2nd person words can be added like, "or if they are reasonably unable to serve I name ____ to serve".

## WILLS SAY "CUSTODIAN" ALSO CAN HOLD AND SPEND A MINOR'S THINGS

Most Wills at their end say Executor may let a person they pick to be "Custodian" manage a minor's property and money, spend it for minor's benefit, and often when minor is 18 or 21 give them the remainder. This is allowed by the new "Uniform Transfers To Minors Act" law that lets a Custodian do what a Guardian does but avoids most costs, work, and court hearings. Trusts are less often used due to this helpful law.

## NAMING A PERSON LIKE A GUARDIAN TO HELP A CHILD RARELY MATTERS

A young child having parents die is rare, so parents naming people like a Guardian to help rarely matters. A study of 311,900 people found 72,240 were under 18 and of these 2014 had lost 1 parent (2.78%) and just 97 both parents (just 0.13%, or 1 in 745), so losing parents is very rare. *Census Life Factors Mortality Study #288*. About half of these children shared common parents so odds for each family are even less.

# CHAPTER 6
# BASIC IDEAS ABOUT HEALTH CARE FORMS

## SOME BASIC IDEAS HELP UNDERSTANDING OF HEALTH CARE LEGAL FORMS

Some ideas help people understand health care forms.

■ By law people controls their own health care by telling medical personnel what they want <u>unless they are</u> <u>"incapacitated"</u> by insufficient ability to a) <u>communicate</u> verbally or by notes, b) be <u>rational</u>, or c) be <u>conscious</u>. Most people keep control of their own care till death or till no big treatment options remain, but some people worry they may be incapacitated a long time so want to do health care forms.

■ Legal documents that help control health care are usually called "Advanced Directives".

■ If an adult 18 or older becomes incapacitated <u>the adult's closest family like spouse or adult child usually</u> <u>can make emergency decisions</u>. But later they usually must then rush to a judge to get further power if no legal document gives them more power over health care.

■ In legal documents a <u>person can be named to have control of health care</u> if needed. This person is often called the "Health Care Agent", "Health Care Attorney-in-Fact", "Health Care Advocate", or a similar name.

■ In legal documents people can <u>write medical instructions that doctors, family, and other people must obey</u>.

■ Parents even without legal documents mostly have <u>full</u> power over health care of <u>children under age 18</u>, and the only exception is teens have some freedom to pick their own family planning or gender related care.

■ Some <u>married people</u> do documents to give a spouse power over medical care if they are incapacitated. Some adults especially <u>to age 25</u> do documents to give this power to parents. The young are less often sick.

■ Pain relief like pain drugs or comfort care is still given even if documents say to stop or limit other care.

■ <u>Most people only do 1 legal document</u> about health care that often names someone to control health care if needed and has a spot for basic instructions (this is sometimes called a "Health Care Power of Attorney").

■ For the rare times stopping health care seems more likely to matter (like due to extreme illness or old age):

-- most people do nothing special and trust family or Health Care Agent to wisely decide when to stop care (they can weigh many factors like pain, cost, likely difficulty of treatment, beliefs, and chances of recovery);

-- a few people do a serious document to say to stop most health care if <u>later</u> doctors think an incapacitated person has very bad health and more medical care likely won't help (sometimes this is called a "Living Will";

-- a few people do a serious document to say <u>starting immediately</u> to not give most medical care (often this is called a "Do-Not-Resuscitate" if about resuscitation, or called a "Physician's Order" if about many treatments).

# CHAPTER 7
# FORM 1: WILL (STANDARD)

## FORM 1 IS A STANDARD WILL THAT IS FLEXIBLE AND WITHOUT A GUARDIAN

Form 1 is a standard Will that is flexible and lets person control some things after their death. This form has no part about a Guardian so this form is for a person with no minor child under age 18.

## FORM IS WILL WITH SEVERAL PARTS

This form at start has place for person doing Will (Testator) to write <u>full legal name</u> unless they dislike it and rarely used it, and write <u>current county or city</u> they reside in (a Will is still valid if people move later).

The 1st paragraph, "Gifts", has many spaces to make either specific gifts of particular property or general gifts like of money. People can delete, copy and paste to add more, or leave blank these gift lines.

The 2nd paragraph, "Separate Writings", says to follow any separate writings done apart from the Will that gifts tangible personal property in way allowed by law.

The 3rd paragraph, "Residue", has a Residue Clause to say any property and money left after other Will parts and any other transfers is gifted to persons as the Residue Clause directs.

The 4th paragraph, "Administration", has space to name an Executor to do some things later.

The 5th paragraph, "Miscellaneous", <u>has paragraphs of helpful language to help with certain legal issues</u>.

Last is paragraph for person doing Will to sign, and paragraph for 2 witnesses to sign and put addresses.

## WILL'S RESIDUE CLAUSE HAS 2 PLACES TO NAME PERSONS TO GET THINGS

In a Will "Residue Clause" any property and money of Testator left after other Will gifts and other things is transferred as the clause directs. Many people use a Residue Clause to gift most things to avoid need to have to describe things and for other helpful legal reasons. In this Will form's Residue Clause there is:

1) a 1st space to name 1 or more persons to get the Residue, and if any named here have not survived and died before the Will maker then any other persons named here take their share,

2) a 2nd space to name people to get things if all in 1st space died before Will maker, and if any people named here didn't survive their shares go to "lineal descendants" like their children.

Most people name in 1st space a spouse or closest family or closest friends, and in 2nd space next closest family or friends. This may seem complicated but usually people in 1st area of Residue Clause get things.

## TESTATOR AND 2 WITNESSES WHILE TOGETHER SIGN WILL

This Will form after being filled out (except bits intentionally left blank) to be valid must be signed by person doing the Will (called Testator) in front of 2 witnesses who then also sign. Testator and witnesses should be in 1 room and see each person sign. To be proper witnesses they must know the document is a Will somehow, and often the Testator says a thing like, "My name is _____ and this is my Will which I do voluntarily and want you 2 people to witness". Witnesses usually do read the 1 paragraph they sign and not the rest of the Will. To be a witness a person must be at least 18, usually not likely to get any property or money though the Will, and usually not named as Executor or Guardian or similar in the Will. Testator need not initial the Will pages. Having Testator and witnesses show each other ID is common but not required.

# LAST WILL AND TESTAMENT

I, _____, of _____, California, do revoke all prior Wills, Testaments, and Codicils, and do make, publish, and declare this as my Will. I am of sound mind and under no duress or undue influence and acting voluntarily.

**1. GIFTS.** I give these gifts in this Will, but to get a gift in this section the recipient must survive me except as otherwise stated below.

I give _____ to _____.

I give _____ to _____.

I give _____ to _____.

I give _____ to _____.

I give _____ to _____.

I give _____ to _____.

I give _____ to _____.

I give _____ to _____.

I give _____ to _____.

**2. SEPARATE WRITINGS.** I may gift tangible personal property by writings separate from this Will as allowed by state law. Such a writing existing when this Will is done is not revoked or canceled unless this Will specifically says this. Such a writing not found within 90 days of my death is canceled and of no effect.

**3. RESIDUE.** I give the residue, rest, and remainder of my estate, my money and property of any kind and nature, and anything I have an interest in so long as it was not transferred by other Will provisions (all of which is called the "residue"), as follows:

a) to _____ who survive me with persons just named who survive me taking the share of non-survivors, then

b) to _____ and if any of those just named do not survive me their part goes to their lineal descendants per stirpes.

**4. ADMINISTRATION.** I name and appoint _____ as Executor including for me, my Will, and my estate.

**5. MISCELLANEOUS.** The following applies to this Will and generally.

It is proper and I request that California law governs this Will and related documents.

Priority of Will gifts of the same type is based on the order they are written.

In this document no unfilled part is a mistake and residue spaces may be left blank.

The words "give" and "gift" also means a devise, bequest, grant, legacy, or similar.

A gift of property no longer owned by Testator at death shall lapse and be of no effect including no payment of money shall be done in its place, all without ademption.

If gift or gift section mentions survival, survive, or surviving then survival is an absolute condition and anti-lapse laws or similar have no effect.

Any failure to make gifts to family including children is intentional and not a mistake.

No gift or transfer made during life reduces or offsets a Will gift unless during my life I expressly usually called it a "loan" or "advancement".

Use of particular gender shall include other genders, reference to singular or plural shall include the other, and "they" may be singular or plural.

Unless parts of this Will specifically say otherwise a secured debt like mortgage or lien on real property or vehicles shall not be paid off, recipient of property takes it subject to liens, and no recipient who has debtor take property or get payment via use or threat of a secured debt may require a devisee, recipient, heir, or estate to pay or do anything.

I give any Executor a) the fullest authority, powers, and discretion allowed by state law, b) authority to lease, sell, mortgage, convey, or retain property including real property in any such manner and time they deem helpful or proper, c) authority to anytime settle or pay claims or debts if they in their sole discretion choose, and d) all other possible power.

An Executor shall not have to give or file annual or other accountings about any money or property including in relation to my Will or estate, and they may act independently in all ways without supervision including through Independent Administration.

Executor is entitled to $900 as compensation for their work and nothing more and not as any fee schedule provides, and I do sincerely thank them for helping me and my estate. I suggest if a lawyer is needed one is hired who charges less than the standard fee schedule.

I request informal or administrative probate of my Will and estate and summary action.

If context permits the terms Executor, Personal Representative, and Administrator shall be interchangeable as if all were written, and if context permits Guardian of any type shall be interchangeable with Conservator and Guardian of Property.

The residue includes lapsed or failed gifts, insurance paid to estate, inheritances owed me, and property I had a power of appointment or testamentary disposition over.

Any Executor, Guardian of any kind, Personal Representative, Conservator, Custodian, and any fiduciary under this Will or otherwise, shall qualify and serve without bond, security, surety, or similar, and despite their residence or lack of connections to a place.

This Will does not revoke a Living Will or any legal document concerning health care.

Any Executor in their sole discretion may transfer money or property of any minor under age 18 at any time to a Custodian under the California Uniform Transfers To Minors Act or any similar law in any place. Custodian will manage, make discretionary payments of any kind and to any recipient to benefit the minor, and pay any remainder to the minor at age 18. I name as Custodian the Guardian of the Estate named in this Will, or if they fail to serve the Executor named in this Will. Executor also may select the Custodian. When doing this no bond, court action, or anything is required of Custodian or Executor.

## TESTATOR

IN WITNESS WHEREOF, I, _____, the Testator, publish, declare, and sign this instrument as my Will this _____ day of _____, 20___, and do hereby declare that I signed this Will while both persons named as Witnesses were present after I asked them to witness my execution of my Will, that I am age 18 or older, that I am now of sound mind and memory, and that I do and execute this Will voluntarily for the purposes expressed in it and not due to duress, menace, fraud or undue influence.

_____
Testator signature

## WITNESSES

On the date written below the Testator named above declared to us persons signing below as Witnesses that this instrument was the Testator's Will, and Testator asked us to witness it and act as Witnesses.

We the persons signing below understand that this instrument is the Testator's Will.

The Testator signed this Will when both of us persons signing below were present.

At the Testator's request, in the Testator's presence, and in the presence of one another, we sign our names as Witnesses.

We believe the Testator is age 18 or older, is of sound mind and memory, and to the best of our knowledge this Will was not procured by duress, menace, fraud or undue influence.

Each of us persons signing below is age 18 or older and is a competent witness.

We declare under penalty of perjury under California law the above is true and correct.

Executed on the ___ day of _____, 20___, in _____, California.

_____          _____
Witness signature                        Witness address


_____          _____
Witness signature                        Witness address

# CHAPTER 8
# FORM 2: WILL (GUARDIAN)

## FORM 2 IS BASIC WILL WITH GUARDIAN CLAUSE FOR YOUNG CHILD

Form 2 is a Will with a Guardian part to be used by a person with a minor child under age 18.

## FORM IS WILL WITH SEVERAL PARTS

This form at start has place for person doing Will (Testator) to write <u>full legal name</u> unless they dislike it and rarely used it, and write <u>current county or city</u> they reside in (a Will is still valid if people move later).

The 1st paragraph, "Gifts", has many spaces to make either specific gifts of particular property or general gifts like of money. People can delete, copy and paste to add more, or leave blank these gift lines.

The 2nd paragraph, "Separate Writings", says to follow any separate writings done apart from the Will that gifts tangible personal property in way allowed by law.

The 3rd paragraph, "Residue", has a Residue Clause to say any property and money left after other Will parts and any other transfers is gifted to persons as the Residue Clause directs.

The 4th paragraph, "Administration", has space to name an Executor to do some things later.

<u>The 5th paragraph, "Guardian", lets Guardian be named to care for any minor child if needed</u> (like if no other parent is available), and also manage child's property and money if needed.

The 6th paragraph, "Miscellaneous", <u>has paragraphs of helpful language to help with certain legal issues</u>.

Last is paragraph for person doing Will to sign, and paragraph for 2 witnesses to sign and put addresses.

## WILL'S RESIDUE CLAUSE HAS 2 PLACES TO NAME PERSONS TO GET THINGS

In a Will "Residue Clause" any property and money of Testator left after other Will gifts and other things is transferred as the clause directs. Many people use a Residue Clause to gift most things to avoid need to have to describe things and for other helpful legal reasons. In this Will form's Residue Clause there is:

1) a 1st space to name 1 or more persons to get the Residue, and if any named here have not survived and died before the Will maker then any other persons named here take their share,

2) a 2nd space to name people to get things if all in 1st space died before Will maker, and if any people named here didn't survive their shares go to "lineal descendants" like their children.

Most people name in 1st space a spouse or closest family or closest friends, and in 2nd space next closest family or friends. This may seem complicated but usually people in 1st area of Residue Clause get things.

## TESTATOR AND 2 WITNESSES WHILE TOGETHER SIGN WILL

This Will form after being filled out (except bits intentionally left blank) to be valid must be signed by person doing the Will (called Testator) in front of 2 witnesses who then also sign. Testator and witnesses should be in 1 room and see each person sign. To be proper witnesses they must know the document is a Will somehow, and often the Testator says a thing like, "My name is _____ and this is my Will which I do voluntarily and want you 2 people to witness". Witnesses usually do read the 1 paragraph they sign and not the rest of the Will. To be a witness a person must be at least 18, usually not likely to get any property or money though the Will, and usually not named as Executor or Guardian or similar in the Will. Testator need not initial the Will pages. Having Testator and witnesses show each other ID is common but not required.

# LAST WILL AND TESTAMENT

I, _____, of _____, California, do revoke all prior Wills, Testaments, and Codicils, and do make, publish, and declare this as my Will. I am of sound mind and under no duress or undue influence and acting voluntarily.

**1. GIFTS.** I give these gifts in this Will, but to get a gift in this section the recipient must survive me except as otherwise stated below.

I give _____ to _____.

I give _____ to _____.

I give _____ to _____.

I give _____ to _____.

I give _____ to _____.

I give _____ to _____.

I give _____ to _____.

I give _____ to _____.

I give _____ to _____.

**2. SEPARATE WRITINGS.** I may gift tangible personal property by writings separate from this Will as allowed by state law. Such a writing existing when this Will is done is not revoked or canceled unless this Will specifically says this. Such a writing not found within 90 days of my death is canceled and of no effect.

**3. RESIDUE.** I give the residue, rest, and remainder of my estate, my money and property of any kind and nature, and anything I have an interest in so long as it was not transferred by other Will provisions (all of which is called the "residue"), as follows:

a) to _____ who survive me with persons just named who survive me taking the share of non-survivors, then

b) to _____ and if any of those just named do not survive me their part goes to their lineal descendants per stirpes.

**4. ADMINISTRATION.** I name and appoint _____ as Executor including for me, my Will, and my estate.

**5. GUARDIAN.** I name _____ as Guardian of the Person with control, authority, and custody of any minor child of mine, and also as Guardian of the Estate with control and authority over any minor child's property, money, and estate.

**6. MISCELLANEOUS.** The following applies to this Will and generally.

It is proper and I request that California law governs this Will and related documents.

Priority of Will gifts of the same type is based on the order they are written.

In this document no unfilled part is a mistake and residue spaces may be left blank.

The words "give" and "gift" also means a devise, bequest, grant, legacy, or similar.

A gift of property no longer owned by Testator at death shall lapse and be of no effect including no payment of money shall be done in its place, all without ademption.

If gift or gift section mentions survival, survive, or surviving then survival is an absolute condition and anti-lapse laws or similar have no effect.

Any failure to make gifts to family including children is intentional and not a mistake.

No gift or transfer made during life reduces or offsets a Will gift unless during my life I expressly usually called it a "loan" or "advancement".

Use of particular gender shall include other genders, reference to singular or plural shall include the other, and "they" may be singular or plural.

Unless parts of this Will specifically say otherwise a secured debt like mortgage or lien on real property or vehicles shall not be paid off, recipient of property takes it subject to liens, and no recipient who has debtor take property or get payment via use or threat of a secured debt may require a devisee, recipient, heir, or estate to pay or do anything.

I give any Executor a) the fullest authority, powers, and discretion allowed by state law, b) authority to lease, sell, mortgage, convey, or retain property including real property in any such manner and time they deem helpful or proper, c) authority to anytime settle or pay claims or debts if they in their sole discretion choose, and d) all other possible power.

An Executor shall not have to give or file annual or other accountings about any money or property including in relation to my Will or estate, and they may act independently in all ways without supervision including through Independent Administration.

Executor is entitled to $900 as compensation for their work and nothing more and not as any fee schedule provides, and I do sincerely thank them for helping me and my estate. I suggest if a lawyer is needed one is hired who charges less than the standard fee schedule.

I request informal or administrative probate of my Will and estate and summary action.

If context permits the terms Executor, Personal Representative, and Administrator shall be interchangeable as if all were written, and if context permits Guardian of any type shall be interchangeable with Conservator and Guardian of Property.

The residue includes lapsed or failed gifts, insurance paid to estate, inheritances owed me, and property I had a power of appointment or testamentary disposition over.

Any Executor, Guardian of any kind, Personal Representative, Conservator, Custodian,

and any fiduciary under this Will or otherwise, shall qualify and serve without bond, security, surety, or similar, and despite their residence or lack of connections to a place.

This Will does not revoke a Living Will or any legal document concerning health care.

Any Executor in their sole discretion may transfer money or property of any minor under age 18 at any time to a Custodian under the California Uniform Transfers To Minors Act or any similar law in any place. Custodian will manage, make discretionary payments of any kind and to any recipient to benefit the minor, and pay any remainder to the minor at age 18. I name as Custodian the Guardian of the Estate named in this Will, or if they fail to serve the Executor named in this Will. Executor also may select the Custodian. When doing this no bond, court action, or anything is required of Custodian or Executor.

## TESTATOR

IN WITNESS WHEREOF, I, _____, the Testator, publish, declare, and sign this instrument as my Will this _____ day of _____, 20___, and do hereby declare that I signed this Will while both persons named as Witnesses were present after I asked them to witness my execution of my Will, that I am age 18 or older, that I am now of sound mind and memory, and that I do and execute this Will voluntarily for the purposes expressed in it and not due to duress, menace, fraud or undue influence.

_____
Testator signature

## WITNESSES

On the date written below the Testator named above declared to us persons signing below as Witnesses that this instrument was the Testator's Will, and Testator asked us to witness it and act as Witnesses.

We the persons signing below understand that this instrument is the Testator's Will.

The Testator signed this Will when both of us persons signing below were present.

At the Testator's request, in the Testator's presence, and in the presence of one another, we sign our names as Witnesses.

We believe the Testator is age 18 or older, is of sound mind and memory, and to the best of our knowledge this Will was not procured by duress, menace, fraud or undue influence.

Each of us persons signing below is age 18 or older and is a competent witness.

We declare under penalty of perjury under California law the above is true and correct.

Executed on the ___ day of _____, 20___, in _____, California.

_____        _____
Witness signature                                        Witness address

_____        _____
Witness signature                                        Witness address

# CHAPTER 9
# FORM 3: CALIFORNIA STATUTORY WILL

## FORM IS WILL WRITTEN INTO LAW THAT'S SIMPLE AND EASY BUT INFLEXIBLE

The California Statutory Will, often just called the "Statutory Will", is a Will written in state law for people to find and use if wanted.  Some California law schools and courts have this on their website. This Will is not flexible but some people like it because it is simple and well known by judges.

## FORM SHOULD NOT BE MODIFIED AND SHOULD BE FILLED OUT BY HAND

This Will is provided for by state law at Cal. Probate Code § 6240.  None of its words can be deleted or modified and it should be filled out by hand by the person doing the Will.

## WILL FORM HAS PARTS THAT CAN MAKE SOME GIFTS

This Will form lets a person make several gifts.  In paragraphs 2 to 5 a person selects from several gift options by writing an "X" or check mark to the left of an option, and **also** signing in box to right of the option. A person in the Will form can name who gets their primary home (paragraph 2), who gets their other property (paragraph 3), who gets their cash (paragraph 4), and who gets anything left ("the balance") (paragraph 5). Or instead of doing all these gifts many people skip paragraphs 2, 3, and 4 and just use paragraph 5 to say who gets anything left.  Many people name the same 1 person or group of people to get all things.

## IN WILL CAN NAME EXECUTOR, GUARDIAN, AND CUSTODIAN

In the Will form a person can name an Executor to handle things after a death (paragraph 9), and also say no costly "bond" is needed to insure them since it uses up estate assets and usually they are trusted. A person using the Will form with no young child under 18 can skip next parts on a Guardian and Custodian. In this Will form a person can be named to be "Guardian" of a child of Testator under age 18 (paragraph 6). And in this Will form a person can be named to be "Custodian" (paragraph 7) to manage property and money of a child under 18 of Testator, and decide how to spend it on child's living costs, health care, and schooling. Then at the age picked in the Will form (often 18 but sometimes 25) anything left is handed over to the child. Note, if a Custodian is not named to manage a child's property and money then this is done by a Guardian which can increase costs and paperwork.

## COMPLETE WILL BY SIGNING WITH 2 WITNESSES

The Statutory Will form is completed by the person doing the Will signing it in front of 2 people acting as witnesses who sign too.  Witnesses should write in the Will where they live in the place provided for this. To be valid witnesses they must know it is a Will, and usually the person doing the Will says it is their Will to witnesses and ask them to witness it.   Witnesses can be anyone 18 or older but usually shouldn't be getting property or money in the Will, and it is better if they're not named to be Executor, Guardian, Custodian, or to other position in the Will.  Having Testator and witnesses show each other ID is common but not required.

# California Statutory Will
## California Probate Code, Section 6240

## INSTRUCTIONS

1. READ THE WILL. Read the whole Will first. If you do not understand something, ask a lawyer to explain it to you.

2. FILL IN THE BLANKS. Fill in the blanks. Follow the instructions in the form carefully. Do not add any words to the Will (except for filling in blanks) or cross out any words.

3. DATE AND SIGN THE WILL AND HAVE TWO WITNESSES SIGN IT. Date and sign the Will and have two witnesses sign it. You and the witnesses should read and follow the Notice to Witnesses found at the end of this Will.

### CALIFORNIA STATUTORY WILL OF

| |
|---|
| Print Your Full Name |
| |

1. <u>Will.</u> This is my Will. I revoke all prior Wills and codicils.

2. <u>Specific Gift of Personal Residence.</u> (Optional-use only if you want to give your personal residence to a different person or persons than you give the balance of your assets to under paragraph 5 below.) I give my interest in my principal personal residence at the time of my death (subject to mortgages and liens) as follows:

(Select one choice only and sign in the box after your choice.)

a. <u>Choice One:</u> All to my spouse or domestic partner, registered with the California Secretary of State, if my spouse or domestic partner, registered with the California Secretary of State, survives me; otherwise to my descendants (my children and the descendants of my children) who survive me.

b. <u>Choice Two:</u> Nothing to my spouse or domestic partner, registered with the California Secretary of State; all to my descendants (my children and the descendants of my children) who survive me.

c. <u>Choice Three:</u> All to the following person if he or she survives me (Insert the name of the person.):

_____

d. <u>Choice Four:</u> Equally among the following persons who survive me (Insert the names of two or more persons.):

_____
_____
_____
_____

3. <u>Specific Gift of Automobiles, Household and Personal Effects.</u> (Optional-use only if you want to give automobiles and household and personal effects to a different person or persons than you give the balance of your assets to under paragraph 5 below.) I give all of my automobiles (subject to loans), furniture, furnishings, household items, clothing, jewelry, and other tangible articles of a personal nature at the time of my death as follows:

(Select one choice only and sign in the box after your choice.)

a. <u>Choice One:</u> All to my spouse or domestic partner, registered with the California Secretary of State, if my spouse or domestic partner, registered with the California Secretary of State, survives me; otherwise to my descendants (my children and the descendants of my children) who survive me.

b. <u>Choice Two:</u> Nothing to my spouse or domestic partner, registered with the California Secretary of State; all to my descendants (my children and the descendants of my children) who survive me.

c. <u>Choice Three:</u> All to the following person if he or she survives me (Insert the name of the person.):

_____

d. <u>Choice Four:</u> Equally among the following persons who survive me (Insert the names of two or more persons.):

_____
_____
_____
_____

4. Specific Gifts of Cash. (Optional) I make the following cash gifts to the persons named below who survive me, or to the named charity, and I sign my name in the box after each gift. If I do not sign in the box, I do not make a gift. (Sign in the box after each gift you make.)

| Name of Person or Charity to receive gift (*name one only - please print*) | Amount of Cash Gift |
| --- | --- |
| | _____<br>*Sign your name in this box to make this gift* |
| Name of Person or Charity to receive gift (*name one only - please print*) | Amount of Cash Gift |
| | _____<br>*Sign your name in this box to make this gift* |
| Name of Person or Charity to receive gift (*name one only - please print*) | Amount of Cash Gift |
| | _____<br>*Sign your name in this box to make this gift* |
| Name of Person or Charity to receive gift (*name one only - please print*) | Amount of Cash Gift |
| | _____<br>*Sign your name in this box to make this gift* |
| Name of Person or Charity to receive gift (*name one only - please print*) | Amount of Cash Gift |
| | _____<br>*Sign your name in this box to make this gift* |

5. Balance of My Assets. Except for the specific gifts made in paragraphs 2, 3 and 4 above, I give the balance of my assets as follows:

(Select one choice only and sign in the box after your choice. If I sign in more than one box or if I do not sign in any box, the court will distribute my assets as if I did not make a Will.)

a. Choice One: All to my spouse or domestic partner, registered with the California Secretary of State, if my spouse or domestic partner, registered with the California Secretary of State, survives me; otherwise to my descendants (my children and the descendants of my children) who survive me.

b. Choice Two: Nothing to my spouse or domestic partner, registered with the California Secretary of State; all to my descendants (my children and the descendants of my children) who survive me.

c. Choice Three: All to the following person if he or she survives me (Insert the name of the person.):

_____

d. Choice Four: Equally among the following persons who survive me (Insert the names of two or more persons.):

_____

_____

_____

_____

6. Guardian of the Child's Person. If I have a child under age 18 and the child does not have a living parent at my death, I nominate the individual named below as First Choice as guardian of the person of that child (to raise the child). If the First Choice does not serve, then I nominate the Second Choice, and then the Third Choice, to serve. Only an individual (not a bank or trust company) may serve.

| Name of First Choice for Guardian of the Person |
| --- |
|  |

| Name of Second Choice for Guardian of the Person |
| --- |
|  |

| Name of Third Choice for Guardian of the Person |
| --- |
|  |

7. Special Provision for Property of Persons Under Age 25. (Optional-unless you use this paragraph, assets that go to a child or other person who is under age 18 may be given to the parent of the person, or to the Guardian named in paragraph 6 above as guardian of the person until age 18, and the court will require a bond, and assets that go to a child or other person who is age 18 or older will be given outright to the person. By using this paragraph you may provide that a custodian will hold the assets for the person until the person reaches any age from 18 to 25 which you choose.) If a beneficiary of this Will is under the age chosen below, I nominate the individual or bank or trust company named below as First Choice as custodian of the property. If the First Choice does not serve, then I nominate the Second Choice, and then the Third Choice, to serve.

| Name of First Choice for Custodian of Assets |
| --- |
|  |

| Name of Second Choice for Custodian of Assets |
| --- |
|  |

| Name of Third Choice for Custodian of Assets |
| --- |
|  |

Insert any age from 18 to 25 as the age for the person to receive the property:
(If you do not choose an age, age 18 will apply.)

8. Executor. I nominate the individual or bank or trust company named below as First Choice as executor. If the First Choice does not serve, then I nominate the Second Choice, and then the Third Choice, to serve.

| Name of First Choice for Executor |
| --- |
| Name of Second Choice for Executor |
| Name of Third Choice for Executor |

9. Bond. My signature in this box means a bond is not required for any person named as executor. A bond may be required if I do not sign in this box:

No bond shall be required.

(Notice: You must sign this Will in the presence of two (2) adult witnesses. The witnesses must sign their names in your presence and in each other's presence. You must first read to them the following sentence.)

**This is my Will: I ask the persons who sign below to be my witnesses.**

Signed on_____ at _____, California.
                                    (date)                                               (city)

Signature of Maker of Will

(Notice to Witnesses: Two (2) adults must sign as witnesses. Each witness must read the following clause before signing. The witnesses should not receive assets under this Will.)

Each of us declares under penalty of perjury under the laws of the State of California that the following is true and correct:

a. On the date written below the maker of this Will declared to us that this instrument was the maker's Will and requested us to act as witnesses to it;

b. We understand this is the maker's Will;

c. The maker signed this Will in our presence, all of us being present at the same time;

d. We now, at the maker's request, and in the maker's and each other's presence, sign below as witnesses;

e. We believe the maker is of sound mind and memory;

f. We believe that this Will was not procured by duress, menace, fraud or undue influence;

g. The maker is age 18 or older; and

h. Each of us is now age 18 or older, is a competent witness, and resides at the address set forth after his or her name.


Dated: _____, _____


| Signature of witness | Signature of witness |
|---|---|
| | |

Print name here:                                   Print name here:

_____            _____


Residence address:                               Residence address:

_____            _____

_____            _____


AT LEAST TWO WITNESSES <u>MUST</u> SIGN
NOTARIZATION ALONE IS NOT SUFFICIENT

# CHAPTER 10
# FORM 4: HANDWRITTEN WILL

## FORM LETS WILL SKIP NORMAL 2 WITNESSES IF WILL IS HANDWRITTEN

A "Handwritten Will" (often called a "Holographic Will" by lawyers) is a Will that is easier to do by not needing the usual 2 witnesses see it signed if it is completely handwritten by the person doing the Will.

## HANDWRITTEN WILL WITHOUT WITNESSES IS ALLOWED IN CALIFORNIA

In 27 states including California a person doing a Will can skip having the usual 2 witnesses for a Will if: 1) it is all handwritten by Testator doing Will (not photocopied, typed, computer printed, or handwritten by anyone else), and 2) it is signed. This is called a "Handwritten Will", or often called a "Holographic Will" by lawyers (since Holo means Whole and Graph means Image in the Greek language which lawyers often use). State legislators allow this since handwriting is hard to forge, people may be in emergency or rush, witnesses may be scarce in the countryside or emergencies, it is private, it can be cheap by skipping complexity and people, and it is traditional in old Mexican, French, and rural lands. States with Handwritten Wills have 55% of the U.S. population so these Wills are common, and in these states these are about 5% of all Wills. Lawmakers want people to have this simple option. See states with Handwritten Wills on map below in dark.

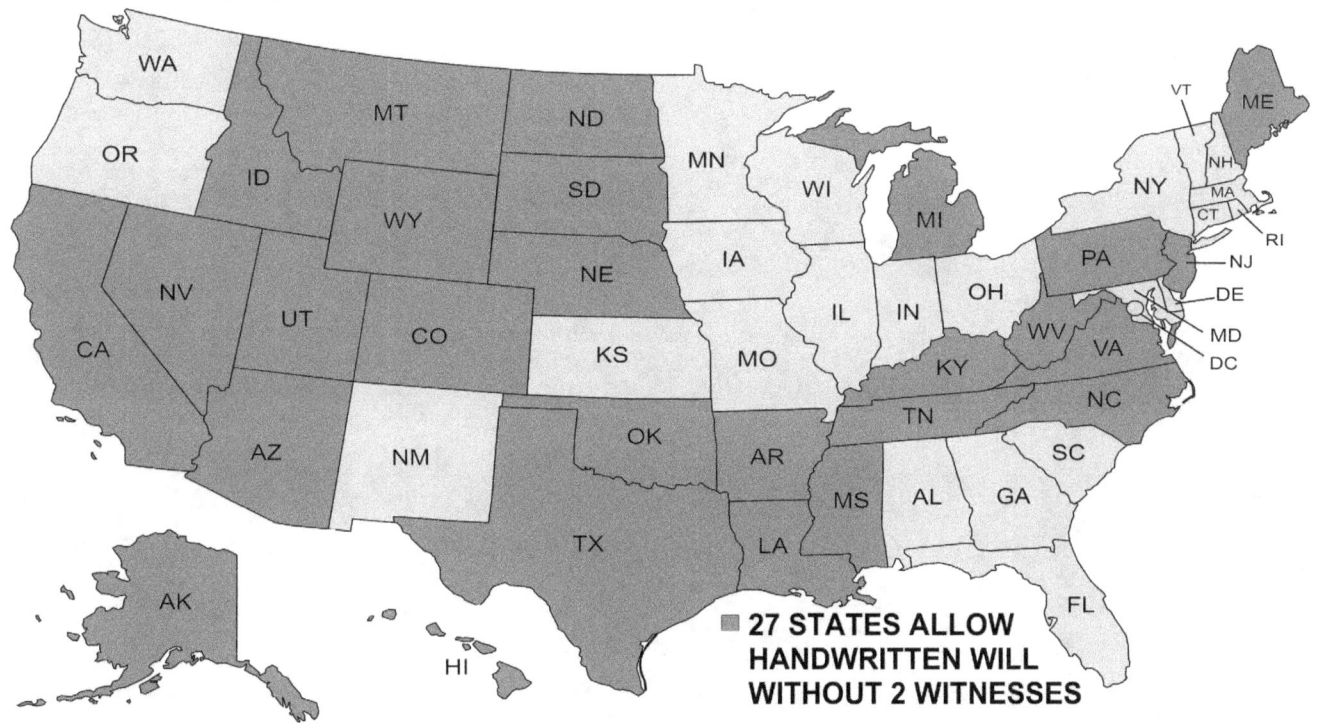

**27 STATES ALLOW HANDWRITTEN WILL WITHOUT 2 WITNESSES**

## HANDWRITTEN WILLS ARE USUALLY FINE BUT REQUIRE LATER WORK

Some lawyers warn Handwritten Wills often read confusingly, skip legal words that can help, and are found invalid more often – but studies show they are liked and fine in most cases. It is true after a death to use a Handwritten Will a family member or friend (or expert) must write an affidavit or say in court the Will looks like Testator's handwriting, which is a minor hassle and sometimes hard to do if a person was a loner. California law does make doing and using a normal Will easy so a Handwritten Will doesn't save much work, for example a normal Will with 2 witnesses can be used later with no further work even if no notary was used. Some people however do choose to do a Handwritten Will especially if they are young, in a hurry, to fix a mistake, to quickly name a Guardian before a trip, after a move to new state, or just temporarily.

# WORDS ON BOTTOM OF PAGE CAN BE USED FOR A HANDWRITTEN WILL

People can do a Handwritten Will with simple words in 1 or 2 sentences that is legal but may leave out helpful parts, for example: "As my Will I give my estate and everything to Judy Smith who shall be Executor." But it is recommended people use more complex words for Handwritten Will shown on bottom of this page. To do this people should change the details and names below on this page to match what they want done. The words below gives things 1st to persons whose names are written in (often spouse or children), then 2nd to surviving descendants (children and grandchildren), and then 3rd to heirs (closest family who by law get things if there's no Will, which is (in order) parents, brothers/sisters, cousins, and then other family). Paragraph 5 below about a Guardian can be totally skipped if a person has no young child under age 18. The Will must be handwritten and signed by person doing Will on some paper and using pencil is allowed.

---

## W I L L

1. My name is David Paul Ax and I now live in Orange County, California. I revoke any prior Wills and Codicils and declare this to be my Will.

2. I give my estate and all else I have to Ann Eve Ax if they survive me. If these people above don't survive me I give all this to my descendants if they survive me. If these people above don't survive me I give all this to my heirs.

3. I name Ann Eve Ax as Executor for me, my Will, and my estate.

4. No bond, surety, or security is required of an Executor or any Guardian.

5. I name Mary Sue Hill as Guardian over the person of any minor child of mine, and over the estate and property of any minor child of mine.

May 8, 2022        David Paul Ax

---

# CHAPTER 11
# FORM 5: TANGIBLE PERSONAL PROPERTY LIST

## LETS GIFTS OF SOME PROPERTY BE EASILY MADE OUTSIDE A WILL
This form lets people outside a Will easily add gifts of some property they want to occur after their death.

## FORM GIVES EASY AND QUICK WAY TO ADD GIFTS
California law lets people before or after a Will has been done in a simple writing say more gifts of some property to occur after their death. This is often called a "Memorandum" or often just called a "List". To be used a Will must say Lists may be done.  If List and Will gift the same item by law the Will is followed. People can do many List pages over time and all can count.  If multiple Lists give the same item the more recently done List controls.  People can modify a List by crossing out or adding words and then signing and dating it.  As explained below a List is mostly limited to giving "tangible personal property".  To reduce legal issues this book's forms say a List not found by someone within 90 days of a person's death is canceled.

---

It may help understanding to show the California law allowing Lists, which in part says:

**Probate Code 6132.**
(a) Notwithstanding any other provision, a will may refer to a writing that directs disposition of tangible personal property not otherwise specifically disposed of by the will, except for money that is common coin or currency and property used primarily in a trade or business. [The following conditions must be met:]
   (1) An unrevoked will refers to the writing.
   (2) The writing is dated and is either in the handwriting of, or signed by, the testator.
   (3) The writing describes the items and the recipients of the property with reasonable certainty[...]

(g) The total value of tangible personal property identified and disposed of in the writing shall not exceed twenty-five thousand dollars ($25,000). If the value of an item [...] exceeds five thousand dollars ($5,000), that item shall not be subject to this section [...]

(h) As used in this section, the following definitions shall apply:
(1) "Tangible personal property" means articles of personal or household use or ornament, including, but not limited to, furniture, furnishings, automobiles, boats, and jewelry, as well as precious metals in any tangible form, such as bullion or coins and articles held for investment purposes.
The term "tangible personal property" does not mean real property, a mobile home as defined in Section 798.3 of the Civil Code, intangible property, such as evidences of indebtedness, bank accounts and other monetary deposits, documents of title, or securities[.]

---

## LIST FORM CAN ONLY GIFT $25,000 OF "TANGIBLE PERSONAL PROPERTY"
The law is a bit confusing but basically Lists can only gift "tangible" things, so touchable items and not accounts, stocks, or things where papers show ownership. Lists can only gift "personal property", so not real property (real estate) or a mobile home.  Lists can't cover any property primarily used in a trade or business. Lists can cover coins or also metals like silver or gold if they are investments and not just plain U.S. money. Often put in a List are furniture, clothing, jewelry, appliances, art, vehicles, and electronics.  Improper items in a List are ignored.  The total value in Lists is limited to $25,000 and no 1 item can have value over $5000.

## TO COMPLETE GIFT LIST A PERSON JUST SIGNS IT
To be valid a List form just must be signed.  Adding a date is helpful and standard.  Usually any Lists are kept with a Will.  People to cancel a List can rip it up, mark it like "void" or "X", or just throw it away.

# TANGIBLE PERSONAL PROPERTY LIST

In this writing are gifts of tangible personal property to occur after my death, but this writing if not found by someone within 90 days of my death is canceled.

I may do many of these writings which should be seen as a single document with the more recent writing controlling if any gifts conflict.

If a person getting a gift below does not survive me such gift is void and canceled.

**PROPERTY ITEMS**                    **NAMES OF RECIPIENTS**

_____ to _____

_____ to _____

_____ to _____

_____ to _____

_____ to _____

_____ to _____

_____ to _____

_____ to _____

_____ to _____

_____ to _____

_____ to _____

_____ to _____

_____ to _____

_____ to _____

_____ to _____

_____ to _____

_____ to _____

DATE:_____        SIGNED:_____

# CHAPTER 12
# FORM 6: ADVANCE HEALTH CARE DIRECTIVE

## FORM LETS PERSON DO THINGS TO AFFECT THEIR LATER HEALTH CARE

This form lets a person write things to affect their later health care. This is often the only Estate Planning form about health care people do. The form is a statutory form found at Cal. Probate Code § 4701, though some people use slightly different forms written by lawyers. The California Attorney General has a nice version of this form that can be filled in on a computer, which can be found at **oag.ca.gov**.

## FORM CAN NAME "AGENT" FOR HEALTH CARE AND GIVE INSTRUCTIONS

The form lets someone be named as "Agent" to control health care if later the person doing the form is incapacitated so can't control health care themselves. This is called the "Power of Attorney" part of form. Often named Agent is spouse, adult child, relative, or friend. Naming a family member as Agent can avoid need to rush to see a judge for power in an emergency. People working for some place giving health care to person doing the form can't be Agent unless they are a family relative. There is a spot to name a second people to serve if needed, but many people skip this since it is rarely needed.

In form a person can give health care instructions, but many people skip this since it's hard to write clearly on all medical issues, and if instructions are unclear medical people may hesitate and wait to talk to a judge.

In some areas of form a person can say when to stop giving care especially if at some future time they are incapacitated and bad health likely won't improve. But most people skip saying when to stop care since this is a hard issue, it rarely matters, and people trust family or Agent to act wisely if needed. Many people call saying when to stop care a "Living Will", and some people use separate documents by a lawyer for this.

In form a person can say who is their primary physician and, also, who should be Conservator to manage their finances if this is ever needed, but many people skip these parts since this information rarely matters.

In form organ donation can be covered but many people skip this since they don't want this, or have handled this as part of their drivers license or state ID application forms (which usually is a better way to do this).

## FORM CAN SAY AGENT SHALL ALSO CONTROL DEAD BODY AND FUNERAL

Agent named in form can be given control of later dead body and related things like funeral, burial, and ceremonies. If this isn't done by law closest family controls this starting with spouse and then adult children. By law people should do funeral and related things a dead person wanted if their money, property, and estate can afford it. In form instructions (limits) can be put, like: "Agent and family do Direct Burial / Direct Cremation (this to save a lot of money takes body and does burial / cremation without family), within week do Wake with snacks at house, use Ivy Cemetery, use small marker, and in month everyone visit grave and do big dinner".

## PERSON SIGNS FORM IN FRONT OF 2 WITNESSES

To complete form a person signs in front of 2 persons acting as witnesses who then sign. A witness can't work for a place giving health care to person doing the form and also can't be named Agent in the form. At least 1 witness can't be related to person doing the form or likely to get things by Will or any similar way.

# ADVANCE HEALTH CARE DIRECTIVE FORM

Probate Code - PROB
DIVISION 4.7. HEALTH CARE DECISIONS [4600 - 4806] ( Division 4.7 added by Stats. 1999, Ch. 658, Sec. 39. )
PART 2. UNIFORM HEALTH CARE DECISIONS ACT [4670 - 4743] ( Part 2 added by Stats. 1999, Ch. 658, Sec. 39. )

CHAPTER 2. Advance Health Care Directive Forms [4700 - 4701] ( Chapter 2 added by Stats. 1999, Ch. 658, Sec. 39. )
4701. The statutory advance health care directive form is as follows:

### ADVANCE HEALTH CARE DIRECTIVE
(California Probate Code Section 4701)
Explanation

You have the right to give instructions about your own health care. You also have the right to name someone else to make health care decisions for you. This form lets you do either or both of these things. It also lets you express your wishes regarding donation of organs and the designation of your primary physician. If you use this form, you may complete or modify all or any part of it. You are free to use a different form.

Part 1 of this form is a power of attorney for health care. Part 1 lets you name another individual as agent to make health care decisions for you if you become incapable of making your own decisions or if you want someone else to make those decisions for you now even though you are still capable. You may also name an alternate agent to act for you if your first choice is not willing, able, or reasonably available to make decisions for you. (Your agent may not be an operator or employee of a community care facility or a residential care facility where you are receiving care, or your supervising health care provider or employee of the health care institution where you are receiving care, unless your agent is related to you or is a coworker.)

Unless the form you sign limits the authority of your agent, your agent may make all health care decisions for you. This form has a place for you to limit the authority of your agent. You need not limit the authority of your agent if you wish to rely on your agent for all health care decisions that may have to be made. If you choose not to limit the authority of your agent, your agent will have the right to:

(a) Consent or refuse consent to any care, treatment, service, or procedure to maintain, diagnose, or otherwise affect a physical or mental condition.

(b) Select or discharge health care providers and institutions.

(c) Approve or disapprove diagnostic tests, surgical procedures, and programs of medication.

(d) Direct the provision, withholding, or withdrawal of artificial nutrition and hydration and all other forms of health care, including cardiopulmonary resuscitation.

(e) Donate your organs, tissues, and parts, authorize an autopsy, and direct disposition of remains.

Part 2 of this form lets you give specific instructions about any aspect of your health care, whether or not you appoint an agent. Choices are provided for you to express your wishes regarding the provision, withholding, or withdrawal of treatment to keep you alive, as well as the provision of pain relief. Space is also provided for you to add to the choices you have made or for you to write out any additional wishes. If you are satisfied to allow your agent to determine what is best for you in making end-of-life decisions, you need not fill out Part 2 of this form.

Part 3 of this form lets you express an intention to donate your bodily organs, tissues, and parts following your death.

Part 4 of this form lets you designate a physician to have primary responsibility for your health care.

After completing this form, sign and date the form at the end. The form must be signed by two qualified witnesses or acknowledged before a notary public. Give a copy of the signed and completed form to your physician, to any other health care providers you may have, to any health care institution at which you are receiving care, and to any health care agents you have named. You should talk to the person you have named as agent to make sure that he or she understands your wishes and is willing to take the responsibility.

You have the right to revoke this advance health care directive or replace this form at any time.

# ADVANCE HEALTH CARE DIRECTIVE FORM

## PART 1
### POWER OF ATTORNEY FOR HEALTH CARE

(1.1)    DESIGNATION OF AGENT:  I designate the following individual as my agent to make health care decisions for me:

_____

(name of individual you choose as agent)

_____    _____  _____  _____

(address)                                               (city)              (state)        (ZIP Code)

_____    _____

(home phone)                                        (work phone)

OPTIONAL:  If I revoke my agent's authority or if my agent is not willing, able, or reasonably available to make a health care decision for me, I designate as my first alternate agent:

_____

(name of individual you choose as first alternate agent)

_____    _____  _____  _____

(address)                                               (city)              (state)        (ZIP Code)

_____    _____

(home phone)                                        (work phone)

OPTIONAL:  If I revoke the authority of my agent and first alternate agent or if neither is willing, able, or reasonably available to make a health care decision for me, I designate as my second alternate agent:

_____

(name of individual you choose as second alternate agent)

_____    _____  _____  _____

(address)                                               (city)              (state)        (ZIP Code)

_____    _____

(home phone)                                        (work phone)

(1.2)    AGENT'S AUTHORITY: My agent is authorized to make all health care decisions for me, including decisions to provide, withhold, or withdraw artificial nutrition and hydration and all other forms of health care to keep me alive, except as I state here:

_____

_____

_____

(Add additional sheets if needed.)

(1.3)    WHEN AGENT'S AUTHORITY BECOMES EFFECTIVE:  My agent's authority becomes effective when my primary physician determines that I am unable to make my own health care decisions unless I mark the following box.
If I mark this box ☐, my agent's authority to make health care decisions for me takes effect immediately.

# ADVANCE HEALTH CARE DIRECTIVE FORM

(1.4.)    AGENT'S OBLIGATION:  My agent shall make health care decisions for me in accordance with this power of attorney for health care, any instructions I give in Part 2 of this form, and my other wishes to the extent known to my agent.  To the extent my wishes are unknown, my agent shall make health care decisions for me in accordance with what my agent determines to be in my best interest.  In determining my best interest, my agent shall consider my personal values to the extent known to my agent.

(1.5)    AGENT'S POSTDEATH AUTHORITY:  My agent is authorized to donate my organs, tissues, and parts, authorize an autopsy, and direct disposition of my remains, except as I state here or in Part 3 of this form:
:

_____

_____

_____

(Add additional sheets if needed.)

(1.6)    NOMINATION OF CONSERVATOR:  If a conservator of my person needs to be appointed for me by a court, I nominate the agent designated in this form.  If that agent is not wiling, able, or reasonably available to act as conservator, I nominate the alternate agents whom I have named, in the order designated.

| PART 2 |
| :---: |
| INSTRUCTIONS FOR HEALTH CARE |

If you fill out this part of the form, you may strike any wording you do not want.

(2.1)    END-OF-LIFE DECISIONS:  I direct that my health care providers and others involved in my care provide, withhold, or withdraw treatment in accordance with the choice I have marked below:

☐   (a) Choice Not to Prolong Life

I do not want my life to be prolonged if (1) I have an incurable and irreversible condition that will result in my death within a relatively short time, (2) I become unconscious and, to a reasonable degree of medical certainty, I will not regain consciousness, or (3) the likely risks and burdens of treatment would outweigh the expected benefits, OR

☐   (b) Choice to Prolong Life

I want my life to be prolonged as long as possible within the limits of generally accepted health care standards.

(2.2)    RELIEF FROM PAIN:  Except as I state in the following space, I direct that treatment for alleviation of pain or discomfort be provided at all times, even if it hastens my death:

_____

_____

(Add additional sheets if needed.)

(2.3)    OTHER WISHES:  (If you do not agree with any of the optional choices above and wish to write your own, or if you wish to add to the instructions you have given above, you may do so here.)  I direct that:

_____

_____

(Add additional sheets if needed.)

## PART 3
## DONATION OF ORGANS, TISSUES, AND PARTS AT DEATH
## (OPTIONAL)

(3.1)  ☐ Upon my death, I give my organs, tissues, and parts (mark box to indicate yes).
By checking the box above, and notwithstanding my choice in Part 2 of this form, I authorize my agent to consent to any temporary medical procedure necessary solely to evaluate and/or maintain my organs, tissues, and/or parts for purposes of donation.

My donation is for the following purposes (strike any of the following you do not want):

      (a) Transplant

      (b) Therapy

      (c) Research

      (d) Education

If you want to restrict your donation of an organ, tissue, or part in some way, please state your restriction on the following lines:

_____

If I leave this part blank, it is not a refusal to make a donation. My state-authorized donor registration should be followed, or, if none, my agent may make a donation upon my death. If no agent is named above, I acknowledge that California law permits an authorized individual to make such a decision on my behalf. (To state any limitation, preference, or instruction regarding donation, please use the lines above or in Section 1.5 of this form).

## PART 4
## PRIMARY PHYSICIAN
## (OPTIONAL)

(4.1)  I designate the following physician as my primary physician:

_____
(name of physician)

_____
(address)                                        (city)                (state)        (ZIP Code)

_____
(phone)

OPTIONAL: If the physician I have designated above is not willing, able, or reasonably available to act as my primary physician, I designate the following physician as my primary physician:

_____
(name of physician)

_____
(address)                                        (city)                (state)        (ZIP Code)

_____
(phone)

## PART 5

(5.1)    EFFECT OF COPY: A copy of this form has the same effect as the original.

(5.2)    SIGNATURE: Sign and date the form here:

_____          _____
(date)                                             (sign your name)

_____          _____
(address)                                          (print your name)

_____
(city) (state)

(5.3)    STATEMENT OF WITNESSES: I declare under penalty of perjury under the laws of California (1) that the individual who signed or acknowledged this advance health care directive is personally known to me, or that the individual's identity was proven to me by convincing evidence (2) that the individual signed or acknowledged this advance directive in my presence, (3) that the individual appears to be of sound mind and under no duress, fraud, or undue influence, (4) that I am not a person appointed as agent by this advance directive, and (5) that I am not the individual's health care provider, an employee of the individual's health care provider, the operator of a community care facility, an employee of an operator of a community care facility, the operator of a residential care facility for the elderly, nor an employee of an operator of a residential care facility for the elderly.

|                  First witness                  |                 Second witness                 |
|-------------------------------------------------|------------------------------------------------|
| _____                  | _____                 |
| (print name)                                    | (print name)                                    |
| _____                  | _____                 |
| (address)                                       | (address)                                       |
| _____                  | _____                 |
| (city)                (state)                   | (city)                (state)                   |
| _____                  | _____                 |
| (signature of witness)                          | (signature of witness)                          |
| _____                  | _____                 |
| (date)                                          | (date)                                          |

(5.4)    ADDITIONAL STATEMENT OF WITNESSES: At least one of the above witnesses must also sign the following declaration:

I further declare under penalty of perjury under the laws of California that I am not related to the individual executing this advance health care directive by blood, marriage, or adoption, and to the best of my knowledge, I am not entitled to any part of the individual's estate upon his or her death under a will now existing or by operation of law.

_____          _____
(signature of witness)                             (signature of witness)

# ADVANCE HEALTH CARE DIRECTIVE FORM

## PART 6
## SPECIAL WITNESS REQUIREMENT

(6.1)    The following statement is required only if you are a patient in a skilled nursing facility--a health care facility that provides the following basic services:  skilled nursing care and supportive care to patients whose primary need is for availability of skilled nursing care on an extended basis.  The patient advocate or ombudsman must sign the following statement:

### STATEMENT OF PATIENT ADVOCATE OR OMBUDSMAN

I declare under penalty of perjury under the laws of California that I am a patient advocate or ombudsman as designated by the State Department of Aging and that I am serving as a witness as required by Section 4675 of the Probate Code.

_____          _____
(date)                                                           (sign your name)


_____          _____
(address)                                                     (print your name)


_____
(city) (state)

(Amended by Stats. 2018, Ch. 287, Sec. 1. (AB 3211) Effective January 1, 2019.)

# CHAPTER 13
# FORM 7: PHYSICIAN ORDERS FOR
# LIFE-SUSTAINING TREATMENT

## FORM SAYS STARTING IMMEDIATELY DO NOT TRY SOME HEALTH CARE

The Physician Orders For Life Sustaining Treatment, often called the "P.O.L.S.T." form, says starting immediately that health care people should not try some health care listed in the form. This form is rarely used and usually only by sickest or oldest people, and it only matters if a person is later incapacitated. The form is short and can be read fast (like by paramedics) and is often used outside a hospital or other facility, but it can be used inside these places too. Most states have similar but slightly different forms. This form covers several medical options and in California is mostly replacing the old Do Not Resuscitate form about only resuscitation, and the P.O.L.S.T. form is often wrongly called the Do Not Resuscitate form.

## CAN SAY TO IMMEDIATELY NO LONGER TRY CERTAIN HEALTH CARE

In the form a person can say starting immediately certain medical care shouldn't be tried if they're later incapacitated and health personnel are deciding what care to give. This form is rarely done, usually only if a person's health is bad like they're in a terminal condition or may soon not regain good consciousness. The form can say to not try to "resuscitate" to help a person's heart or breathing (which covers many things like cardio-pulmonary resuscitation (C.P.R.) which is pressing chest and lightly blowing air in lungs, electric shock to restart heart or get stable heartbeat, and forcing air into lungs by tube or machines). The form can also say to not try several other medical treatments. A doctor often helps explain the form. Some hospitals and other places have their own form they prefer be used.

## FORM IS SIGNED BY PERSON DOING THE FORM AND A DOCTOR

The form must be signed by person doing the form or someone with authority for them, and also signed by a doctor or similar health professional (they often help explain why this form is not wise to do). Once done the form should be shown to places that may give care to be put in a person's medical file. Some people keeps the form handy to show paramedics or other people who may want to give care. Some people keep the form on a bedside table, home refrigerator, in shirt pocket, or wear a bracelet or similar made by companies chosen by the state. A person with capacity still thinking fine can override this form like by saying this to doctors or not showing form to paramedics. To cancel the form a person should tell all places shown the form it is canceled.

# Physician Orders for Life-Sustaining Treatment (POLST)

**First follow these orders, then contact Physician/ NP/ PA.** A copy of the signed POLST form is a legally valid physician order. Any section not completed implies full treatment for that section. **POLST complements an Advance Directive and is not intended to replace that document.**

EMSA #111 B
(Effective 4/1/2017)*

| Patient Last Name: | Date Form Prepared: |
|---|---|
| Patient First Name: | Patient Date of Birth: |
| Patient Middle Name: | Medical Record #: *(optional)* |

---

## A
*Check One*

**CARDIOPULMONARY RESUSCITATION (CPR):** *If patient has no pulse and is not breathing.*
*If patient is NOT in cardiopulmonary arrest, follow orders in Sections B and C.*

☐ **Attempt Resuscitation/CPR** (Selecting CPR in Section A **requires** selecting Full Treatment in Section B)

☐ **Do Not Attempt Resuscitation/DNR** (Allow Natural Death)

---

## B
*Check One*

**MEDICAL INTERVENTIONS:** *If patient is found with a pulse and/or is breathing.*

☐ **Full Treatment – primary goal of prolonging life by all medically effective means.**
In addition to treatment described in Selective Treatment and Comfort-Focused Treatment, use intubation, advanced airway interventions, mechanical ventilation, and cardioversion as indicated.
  ☐ *Trial Period of Full Treatment.*

☐ **Selective Treatment** – goal of treating medical conditions while avoiding burdensome measures.
In addition to treatment described in Comfort-Focused Treatment, use medical treatment, IV antibiotics, and IV fluids as indicated. Do not intubate. May use non-invasive positive airway pressure. Generally avoid intensive care.
  ☐ *Request transfer to hospital **only** if comfort needs cannot be met in current location.*

☐ **Comfort-Focused Treatment** – primary goal of maximizing comfort.
Relieve pain and suffering with medication by any route as needed; use oxygen, suctioning, and manual treatment of airway obstruction. Do not use treatments listed in Full and Selective Treatment unless consistent with comfort goal. *Request transfer to hospital **only** if comfort needs cannot be met in current location.*

Additional Orders: _____
_____

---

## C
*Check One*

**ARTIFICIALLY ADMINISTERED NUTRITION:** *Offer food by mouth if feasible and desired.*

☐ Long-term artificial nutrition, including feeding tubes.  Additional Orders: _____
☐ Trial period of artificial nutrition, including feeding tubes. _____
☐ No artificial means of nutrition, including feeding tubes. _____

---

## D

**INFORMATION AND SIGNATURES:**

Discussed with:  ☐ Patient (Patient Has Capacity)     ☐ Legally Recognized Decisionmaker

☐ Advance Directive dated _____, available and reviewed →
☐ Advance Directive not available
☐ No Advance Directive

Health Care Agent if named in Advance Directive:
Name: _____
Phone: _____

**Signature of Physician / Nurse Practitioner / Physician Assistant** (Physician/NP/PA)
My signature below indicates to the best of my knowledge that these orders are consistent with the patient's medical condition and preferences.

| Print Physician/NP/PA Name: | Physician/NP/PA Phone #: | Physician/PA License #, NP Cert. #: |
|---|---|---|
| Physician/NP/PA Signature: *(required)* | | Date: |

**Signature of Patient or Legally Recognized Decisionmaker**
I am aware that this form is voluntary. By signing this form, the legally recognized decisionmaker acknowledges that this request regarding resuscitative measures is consistent with the known desires of, and with the best interest of, the individual who is the subject of the form.

| Print Name: | | Relationship: *(write self if patient)* |
|---|---|---|
| Signature: *(required)* | Date: | Your POLST may be added to a secure electronic registry to be accessible by health providers, as permitted by HIPAA. |
| Mailing Address (street/city/state/zip): | Phone Number: | |

**SEND FORM WITH PATIENT WHENEVER TRANSFERRED OR DISCHARGED**

*Form versions with effective dates of 1/1/2009, 4/1/2011, 10/1/2014 or 01/01/2016 are also valid

## Patient Information

| Name (last, first, middle): | Date of Birth: | Gender:<br>M    F |
|---|---|---|

| **NP/PA's Supervising Physician** | **Preparer Name** (if other than signing Physician/NP/PA) | |
|---|---|---|
| Name: | Name/Title: | Phone #: |

## Additional Contact          □ None

| Name: | Relationship to Patient: | Phone #: |
|---|---|---|

## Directions for Health Care Provider

### Completing POLST

- **Completing a POLST form is voluntary.** California law requires that a POLST form be followed by healthcare providers, and provides immunity to those who comply in good faith. In the hospital setting, a patient will be assessed by a physician, or a nurse practitioner (NP) or a physician assistant (PA) acting under the supervision of the physician, who will issue appropriate orders that are consistent with the patient's preferences.
- **POLST does not replace the Advance Directive**. When available, review the Advance Directive and POLST form to ensure consistency, and update forms appropriately to resolve any conflicts.
- POLST must be completed by a health care provider based on patient preferences and medical indications.
- A legally recognized decisionmaker may include a court-appointed conservator or guardian, agent designated in an Advance Directive, orally designated surrogate, spouse, registered domestic partner, parent of a minor, closest available relative, or person whom the patient's physician/NP/PA believes best knows what is in the patient's best interest and will make decisions in accordance with the patient's expressed wishes and values to the extent known.
- A legally recognized decisionmaker may execute the POLST form only if the patient lacks capacity or has designated that the decisionmaker's authority is effective immediately.
- To be valid a POLST form must be signed by (1) a physician, or by a nurse practitioner or a physician assistant acting under the supervision of a physician and within the scope of practice authorized by law and (2) the patient or decisionmaker. Verbal orders are acceptable with follow-up signature by physician/NP/PA in accordance with facility/community policy.
- If a translated form is used with patient or decisionmaker, attach it to the signed English POLST form.
- Use of original form is strongly encouraged. Photocopies and FAXes of signed POLST forms are legal and valid. A copy should be retained in patient's medical record, on Ultra Pink paper when possible.

### Using POLST

- Any incomplete section of POLST implies full treatment for that section.

*Section A:*

- If found pulseless and not breathing, no defibrillator (including automated external defibrillators) or chest compressions should be used on a patient who has chosen "Do Not Attempt Resuscitation."

*Section B:*

- When comfort cannot be achieved in the current setting, the patient, including someone with "Comfort-Focused Treatment," should be transferred to a setting able to provide comfort (e.g., treatment of a hip fracture).
- Non-invasive positive airway pressure includes continuous positive airway pressure (CPAP), bi-level positive airway pressure (BiPAP), and bag valve mask (BVM) assisted respirations.
- IV antibiotics and hydration generally are not "Comfort-Focused Treatment."
- Treatment of dehydration prolongs life. If a patient desires IV fluids, indicate "Selective Treatment" or "Full Treatment."
- Depending on local EMS protocol, "Additional Orders" written in Section B may not be implemented by EMS personnel.

### Reviewing POLST

It is recommended that POLST be reviewed periodically. Review is recommended when:

- The patient is transferred from one care setting or care level to another, or
- There is a substantial change in the patient's health status, or
- The patient's treatment preferences change.

### Modifying and Voiding POLST

- A patient with capacity can, at any time, request alternative treatment or revoke a POLST by any means that indicates intent to revoke. It is recommended that revocation be documented by drawing a line through Sections A through D, writing "VOID" in large letters, and signing and dating this line.
- A legally recognized decisionmaker may request to modify the orders, in collaboration with the physician/NP/PA, based on the known desires of the patient or, if unknown, the patient's best interests.

This form is approved by the California Emergency Medical Services Authority in cooperation with the statewide POLST Task Force. For more information or a copy of the form, visit www.caPOLST.org.

# CHAPTER 14
# FORM 8: UNIFORM STATUTORY FORM POWER OF ATTORNEY

## FORM LETS POWER BE GIVEN OVER PROPERTY, MONEY, AND MORE

This form lets person during life give power to someone trusted over property, money, and other things. This is a statutory form that is provided for in state law at Cal. Probate Code § 4401. Several websites have an online version of form that can be filled in online, like **lacounty.gov** or **disasterlegalservicesca.org**.

## FORM GIVES POWER TO LET SOMEONE CONTROL PROPERTY AND MONEY

Form lets a person give power to someone trusted over their money, property, records, and other things. In form the person giving power is called "Principal" and person getting power called "Agent" (often called an "Attorney-in-Fact") who is often a spouse, relative, or friend. This can lets someone help if a person is sick, busy, or away. It can let Agent pay bills, use accounts, buy or sell items, sign contracts, hire workers, borrow, and get records. A person who is not incapacitated can overrule or fire the Agent so really power is shared. The form is called "durable" since it still has power if the person who did the form is later incapacitated. When using form a signature should be like: "Ed Doe signing as agent under Power of Attorney for Ann Wu". Importantly, in the form a person can mark which powers they want to give by initialing certain form lines. Most people give Agent much or all powers (like by initially in form item "N") since banks and others may not obey Agent if it is unclear if they have power to do a thing. Some people write more to give more power, like write: "My Agent has full general power and can do all things and acts I could do if personally present".

## IN FORM CAN NAME OTHER PERSONS

Though rare people can write in 2 persons to be Agent and then say how they should act, like write either: "All Agents must agree and both join in any act" or "Agent may act separately without other person". Though rarely needed some people modify form to add fallback person for Agent, like: "If Agent fails to act I appoint as my first alternate to be Agent:_____". In case major help managing finances is needed later people can modify form to name Agent to also be Conservator, like: "I name the person named Agent to be Conservator if needed to serve without bond and with all independent powers in Cal. Probate Code § 2591".

## DUE TO RISKS INCLUDING FRAUD MANY SKIP FORM OR CONSULT A LAWYER

Using this form can be risky and lead to loss of money and property since the Agent can do harmful things like buy unneeded or costly items, embezzle or steal, or let other people do harm. Agents have a duty to act reasonably for Principal but later may be out of money later so can't pay to undo their harm. Usually banks or others can't be blamed for obeying an Agent, and if they hesitate to obey they may owe a small money fine. The law is complex and basic acts may be fine like paying bills, getting records, or moving funds, but other acts may be improper like gifts to anyone, risky investments, or uncommon things. It is best if a person not their Agent does anything unusual. Many people skip the form or first see a lawyer.

## PERSON SIGNS FORM IN FRONT OF A NOTARY

The form must be signed in front of a notary who notarizes and signs it too. Once it is done most people give form to person getting power to use, and some cautious people show it to banks and others in advance. To cancel the form a person should take back copies and usually inform places that saw it that it's canceled.

# UNIFORM STATUTORY FORM POWER OF ATTORNEY

(California Probate Code Section 4401)

NOTICE: THE POWERS GRANTED BY THIS DOCUMENT ARE BROAD AND SWEEPING. THEY ARE EXPLAINED IN THE UNIFORM STATUTORY FORM POWER OF ATTORNEY ACT (CALIFORNIA PROBATE CODE SECTIONS 4400-4465). THE POWERS LISTED IN THIS DOCUMENT DO NOT INCLUDE ALL POWERS THAT ARE AVAILABLE UNDER THE PROBATE CODE. ADDITIONAL POWERS AVAILABLE UNDER THE PROBATE CODE MAY BE ADDED BY SPECIFICALLY LISTING THEM UNDER THE SPECIAL INSTRUCTIONS SECTION OF THIS DOCUMENT. IF YOU HAVE ANY QUESTIONS ABOUT THESE POWERS, OBTAIN COMPETENT LEGAL ADVICE. THIS DOCUMENT DOES NOT AUTHORIZE ANYONE TO MAKE MEDICAL AND OTHER HEALTH-CARE DECISIONS FOR YOU. YOU MAY REVOKE THIS POWER OF ATTORNEY IF YOU LATER WISH TO DO SO.

I _____
(your name and address)

appoint _____
(name and address of the person appointed, or of each person appointed if you want to designate more than one)

as my agent (attorney-in-fact) to act for me in any lawful way with respect to the following initialed subjects:

TO GRANT ALL OF THE FOLLOWING POWERS, INITIAL THE LINE IN FRONT OF (N) AND IGNORE THE LINES IN FRONT OF THE OTHER POWERS.

TO GRANT ONE OR MORE, BUT FEWER THAN ALL, OF THE FOLLOWING POWERS, INITIAL THE LINE IN FRONT OF EACH POWER YOU ARE GRANTING.

TO WITHHOLD A POWER, DO NOT INITIAL THE LINE IN FRONT OF IT. YOU MAY, BUT NEED NOT, CROSS OUT EACH POWER WITHHELD.

INITIAL

_____ (A)  Real property transactions.

_____ (B)  Tangible personal property transactions.

_____ (C)  Stock and bond transactions.

_____ (D)  Commodity and option transactions.

_____ (E)  Banking and other financial institution transactions.

_____ (F)  Business operating transactions.

_____ (G)  Insurance and annuity transactions.

_____ (H)  Estate, trust, and other beneficiary transactions.

_____ (I)  Claims and litigation.

_____ (J)  Personal and family maintenance.

_____ (K)  Benefits from social security, medicare, medicaid, or other governmental programs, or civil or military service.

_____ (L)  Retirement plan transactions.

_____ (M)  Tax matters.

_____ (N)  ALL OF THE POWERS LISTED ABOVE.

**YOU NEED NOT INITIAL ANY OTHER LINES IF YOU INITIAL LINE (N).**

## SPECIAL INSTRUCTIONS:

ON THE FOLLOWING LINES YOU MAY GIVE SPECIAL INSTRUCTIONS LIMITING OR EXTENDING THE POWERS GRANTED TO YOUR AGENT.

_____
_____
_____
_____
_____
_____
_____
_____
_____
_____
_____
_____
_____
_____
_____
_____
_____
_____
_____
_____

UNLESS YOU DIRECT OTHERWISE ABOVE, THIS POWER OF ATTORNEY IS EFFECTIVE IMMEDIATELY AND WILL CONTINUE UNTIL IT IS REVOKED.

This power of attorney will continue to be effective even though I become incapacitated.

STRIKE THE PRECEDING SENTENCE IF YOU DO NOT WANT THIS POWER OF ATTORNEY TO CONTINUE IF YOU BECOME INCAPACITATED.

## EXERCISE OF POWER OF ATTORNEY WHERE
## MORE THAN ONE AGENT DESIGNATED

If I have designated more than one agent, the agents are to act

_____

IF YOU APPOINTED MORE THAN ONE AGENT AND YOU WANT EACH AGENT TO BE ABLE TO ACT ALONE WITHOUT THE OTHER AGENT JOINING, WRITE THE WORD "SEPARATELY" IN THE BLANK SPACE ABOVE. IF YOU DO NOT INSERT ANY WORD IN THE BLANK SPACE, OR IF YOU INSERT THE WORD "JOINTLY", THEN ALL OF YOUR AGENTS MUST ACT OR SIGN TOGETHER.

I agree that any third party who receives a copy of this document may act under it. A third party may seek identification. Revocation of the power of attorney is not effective as to a third party until the third party has actual knowledge of the revocation. I agree to indemnify the third party for any claims that arise against the third party because of reliance on this power of attorney.

Signed this _____ day of _____, 20_____.

_____
(your signature)

State of _____    County of _____

BY ACCEPTING OR ACTING UNDER THE APPOINTMENT, THE AGENT ASSUMES THE FIDUCIARY AND OTHER LEGAL RESPONSIBILITIES OF AN AGENT.

## ACKNOWLEDGEMENT

STATE OF CALIFORNIA                    )
                                       ) ss.
COUNTY OF _____         )

On the _____ day of _____, 20___, before me, _____, Notary Public, personally appeared _____, Principal, who proved to me on the basis of satisfactory evidence to be the person(s) whose name(s) is/are subscribed to the within instrument and acknowledged to me that he/she/they executed the same in his/her/their authorized capacity(ies), and that by his/her/their signature(s) on the instrument the person(s), or the entity upon behalf of which the person(s) acted, executed the instrument.

I certify under PENALTY OF PERJURY under the laws of the State of California that the foregoing paragraph is true and correct.

WITNESS my hand and official seal.

Signature: _____        (Seal)

# CHAPTER 15
# FORM 9: AUTHORIZATION TO CONSENT TO MEDICAL TREATMENT OF A MINOR

## FORM LETS PARENT/GUARDIAN SHARE CONTROL OF CHILD'S HEALTH CARE

This form lets parent or guardian of a child under 18 name someone to have power to make health care decisions for child in case this is ever needed.

## FORM CAN GIVE POWER OVER HEALTH CARE OF CHILD UNDER 18

California helpfully lets a parent or guardian give power over health care of a child under 18 to someone named in the form in case this may be helpful later. Cal. Family Code § 6910 allowing this says:

"The parent, guardian, or caregiver of a minor who is a relative of the minor and who may authorize medical care and dental care under Section 6550, may authorize in writing an adult into whose care a minor has been entrusted to consent to medical care or dental care, or both, for the minor."

This form may help if a child falls sick and a relative, friend, teacher, or coach near the child needs to quickly authorize medical care. This form is sometimes used if a parent or child is away from the other for work, school, drug treatment, sports, prison or jail, immigration, military, month long visit with family or friends, or if child is very sick in hospital and needs person close by to make quick decisions. The form is usually not done for brief situations like babysitting daycare, week with relative, or any case a parent can come quickly. The parent or guardian who did the form can fire a person or overrule a decision so really power is shared. If wanted people can modify the form to say it ends at a certain date but most people do not bother with this.

## SOME MODIFY POWER OF ATTORNEY TO GIVE MORE POWER OVER CHILD

Some people especially if child may be outside California also modify a Power of Attorney form to make clear power over a child is given in that form, like by writing: "I specifically name _____ as Attorney-in-Fact with full power and authority over my child under age 18 (including over health care, dental, school, and all other things), and this child is named and was born as follows:_____". If parents will be away a long time they may have lawyer do a fancy version of this or do other legal actions. A Power of Attorney form is usually notarized and many states outside California require this to control matters involving a minor child.

## FORM IS SIGNED BY PARENT OR GUARDIAN

The form to be valid just must be signed by a parent or guardian. Some people use a notary to be extra careful or if the child may be outside California where often a notary is needed to give power of a child. Some people modify form to add the 2nd parent to make it likelier other people trust the form. Once done some cautious people quickly show form to schools and doctors in advance to say they should follow it later. Once it is completed and signed usually people give form to person getting power to use if ever needed. To cancel the form a person should take back copies and usually tell places shown the form it is canceled. Note, if no parent is available and another adult is living with and caring for A child that adult usually can sign a "Caregiver Affidavit" to get power over health care and schooling.

# AUTHORIZATION TO CONSENT TO MEDICAL TREATMENT OF A MINOR

## (California Family Code Section 6910)

I, the undersigned, hereby give power and authority to the following person, who is an adult into whose care the minor named below have been entrusted:

Name: _____ Phone:_____

Address:_____

I give this person power and authority to consent, agree, and authorize any scan, test, X-ray, examination, anesthesia, diagnosis, medical treatment, hospital care, transport or admission to a hospital or any other place, dental procedure, food, surgery, or any other similar thing, for and over the following minor(s):

Minor's Name: _____ Date of birth:_____

Minor's Name: _____ Date of birth:_____

Minor's Name: _____ Date of birth:_____

It is understood that this authorization is given in advance of any specific diagnosis, treatment, or hospital care being required, but is given to provide authority to the above-named person to give specific consent to any and all such diagnosis, treatment, or hospital care which a doctor or any health care professional may deem advisable.

I authorizes any hospital, other facility, or other party that has treated the minor to surrender physical custody to the above named authorized party.

My relation with the minor(s) is:     [     ] parent with legal custody
                                      [     ] guardian with legal custody
                                      [     ] other:_____

This authorization is made under California Family Code § 6910.


Signed:_____ Dated:_____

Print Name:_____ Phone:_____

Address:_____

# APPENDIX: SAMPLE FILLED OUT FORMS

TO GET FORMS TO USE PEOPLE CAN:

(1) PHOTOCOPY BOOK PAGES,

(2) TEAR OUT PAGES FROM A BOOK, OR

(3) DOWNLOAD BOOK WITH FORMS FROM WWW.DAVENPORTPUBLISHING.COM AND USUALLY PDF FORM AT IS BEST TO AVOID SPACING/FORMAT CHANGES, AND THEN PEOPLE JUST HANDWRITE ON THE PRINTED OUT DOCUMENT.

EMAIL ANY COMMENTS TO DAVENPORTPRESS@GMAIL.COM .

On the next pages to show how it can be done are some sample filled out legal forms.

People can add words to legal forms by computer or typewriter to be neater, but many people just by hand use pen, marker, or pencil to handwrite words into forms.

It is not required but is bit better if signatures are in ink or marker not pencil.

Many parts of the forms especially Will gifts can be left empty and unfilled.

Anyone can fill in words in legal form not just the person doing the form, like a friend with neat writing can fill in all the words, addresses, and dates that are needed. Only the final signatures must be done by each person who wants the form.

To add words in form by pen, pencil, typewriter, or computer any of these is fine:
"I appoint ____John Doe____ as Agent" ,
"I appoint ____John Doe____ as Agent",
"I appoint John Doe as Agent".

When doing forms it may help to know "respectively" means "in order just stated".

People need not worry about neatness or small mistakes, and a document is usually fine if those people who knew a decedent in life can tell the likely meaning.

# LAST WILL AND TESTAMENT

I, _Paul Thomas Maxwell_ , of _Los Angeles_ , California, do revoke all prior Wills, Testaments, and Codicils, and do make, publish, and declare this as my Will. I am of sound mind and under no duress or undue influence and acting voluntarily.

**1. GIFTS.** I give these gifts in this Will, but to get a gift in this section the recipient must survive me except as otherwise stated below.

I give _____ to _____.

I give _____ to _____.

I give _____ to _____.

I give _____ to _____.

I give _____ to _____.

I give _____ to _____.

I give _____ to _____.

I give _____ to _____.

I give _____ to _____.

I give _____ to _____.

SKIPPED

**2. SEPARATE WRITINGS.** I may gift tangible personal property by writings separate from this Will as allowed by state law. Such a writing existing when this Will is done is not revoked or canceled unless this Will specifically says this. Such a writing not found within 90 days of my death is canceled and of no effect.

**3. RESIDUE.** I give the rest and residue and remainder of my estate, my money and property of any kind and nature, and anything I have an interest in so long as it was not transferred by other Will provisions (all of which is called the "residue"), as follows:

a) to _Susan Lee Maxwell_ who survive me with persons just named who survive me taking the share of non-survivors, then

b) to _Oscar David Maxwell and Jennifer Judy Tabor_ and if any of those just named do not survive me their part goes to their lineal descendants, per stirpes.

**4. ADMINISTRATION.**  I name and appoint  _Susan Lee Maxwell_  as Executor including for me, my Will, and my estate.

**5. MISCELLANEOUS.**  The following applies to this Will and generally.

As Testator I agree and say I am a California resident and California should apply to this Will and all related issues and matters, and I request this be done.

Priority of Will gifts of the same type is based on the order they are written.

In this document no unfilled part is a mistake and residue spaces may be left blank.

The words "give" and "gift" also means a devise, bequest, grant, legacy, or similar.

A gift of property no longer owned by Testator at death shall lapse and be of no effect including no payment of money shall be done in its place, all without ademption.

If gift or gift section mentions survival, survive, or surviving then survival is an absolute condition and anti-lapse laws or similar have no effect.

Any failure to make gifts to family including children is intentional and not a mistake.

No gift or transfer made during life reduces or offsets a Will gift unless during my life I expressly usually called it a "loan" or "advancement".

Use of particular gender shall include other genders, reference to singular or plural shall include the other, and "they" may be singular or plural.

Unless parts of this Will specifically say otherwise a secured debt like mortgage or lien on real property or vehicles shall not be paid off, recipient of property takes it subject to liens, and no recipient who has debtor take property or get payment via use or threat of a secured debt may require a devisee, recipient, heir, or estate to pay or do anything.

I give any Executor a) the fullest authority, powers, and discretion allowed by state law, b) authority to lease, sell, mortgage, convey, or retain property including real property in any such manner and time they deem helpful or proper, c) authority to anytime settle or pay claims or debts if they in their sole discretion choose, and d) all other possible power.

An Executor shall not have to give or file annual or other accountings about any money or property including in relation to my Will or estate, and they may act independently in all ways without supervision including through Independent Administration.

Executor is entitled to $900 as compensation for their work and nothing more and not as any fee schedule provides, and I do sincerely thank them for helping me and my estate. I suggest if a lawyer is needed one is hired who charges less than the standard fee schedule.

I request informal or administrative probate of my Will and estate and summary action.

Any Executor, Guardian of any kind, Personal Representative, Conservator, Custodian, and any fiduciary under this Will or otherwise, shall qualify and serve without bond, security, surety, or similar, and despite their residence or lack of connections to a place.

This Will does not revoke a Living Will or any legal document concerning health care.

I name as Custodian under the California Uniform Transfers to Minors Act or a similar

Any Executor in their sole discretion may transfer money or property of any minor under age 18 at any time to a Custodian under the California Uniform Transfers To Minors Act or any similar law in any place. Custodian will manage, make discretionary payments of any kind and to any recipient to benefit the minor, and pay any remainder to the minor at age 18. I name as Custodian the Guardian of the Estate named in this Will, or if they fail to serve the Executor named in this Will. Executor also may select the Custodian. When doing this no bond, court action, or anything is required of Custodian or Executor.

## TESTATOR

IN WITNESS WHEREOF, I, _Paul Thomas Maxwell_ , the Testator, publish, declare, and sign this instrument as my Will this _22nd_ day of _June_ , 20_22_ , and do hereby declare that I signed this Will while both persons named as Witnesses were present after I asked them to witness my execution of my Will, that I am age 18 or older, that I am now of sound mind and memory, and that I do and execute this Will voluntarily for the purposes expressed in it and not due to duress, menace, fraud or undue influence.

_Paul Thomas Maxwell_

Testator signature

## WITNESSES

On the date written below the Testator named above declared to us persons signing below as Witnesses that this instrument was the Testator's Will, and Testator asked us to witness it and act as Witnesses.

We the persons signing below understand that this instrument is the Testator's Will.

The Testator signed this Will when both of us persons signing below were present.

At the Testator's request, in the Testator's presence, and in the presence of one another, we sign our names as Witnesses.

We believe the Testator is age 18 or older, is of sound mind and memory, and to the best of our knowledge this Will was not procured by duress, menace, fraud or undue influence.

Each of us persons signing below is age 18 or older and is a competent witness.

We declare under penalty of perjury under California law the above is true and correct.

Executed on the _22nd_ day of _June_ , 20_22_ , at _Bakersfield_ , California.

_Eve Mable Rogers_          _14 2nd St., Fontana, California, 90011_
Witness                               Witness Address

_Mary Ann Moon_          _835 Buffalo Road, Milwaukee, WI 53290_
Witness                               Witness Address

# LAST WILL AND TESTAMENT

I, _____Paul Brian Kent_____, of __Riverside County__, California, do revoke all prior Wills, Testaments, and Codicils, and do make, publish, and declare this as my Will. I am of sound mind and under no duress or undue influence and acting voluntarily.

**1. GIFTS.** I give these gifts in this Will, but to get a gift in this section the recipient must survive me except as otherwise stated below.

I give _big oak table_ to _Anne J. Wix._

I give ___$5,000___ to ___Loretta Marsha Switt_.

I give __63 Ivy Road, Fresno, California__ to __Kenneth Victor Poppler._

I give __all land I own inside city limits of San Diego, California_ to _Greta Olivia Fox_.

I give __903 Iceberg Road, Anchorage, Alaska__ to __James Eric Hanson__.

I give _Bronze Roman Lamp_ to _Anne Kilby__ and __Kevin Kilby._

I give __wedding ring__ to _Ruth Jones._

I give _all jewelry not given above__ to _Kay Pidoski._

I give ___$781.35___ to _Wanda Kay Zinski_.

I give __Wells Fargo acct ending in #8923__ to __Lawrence Deer a hunting buddy_.

I give _1998 Ford truck__ to __John Rupert Smith_.

I give _$200__ to _Binker Food Shelf on Smith Road in Oakland, California_.

I give _all spare tires and auto parts I own_ to _Victor Perez my mechanic_.

I give ___$1000 each___ to __each of my grandchildren__.

**2. SEPARATE WRITINGS.** I may gift tangible personal property by writings separate from this Will as allowed by state law. Such a writing existing when this Will is done is not revoked or canceled unless this Will specifically says this. Such a writing not found within 90 days of my death is canceled and of no effect.

**3. RESIDUE.** I give the rest and residue and remainder of my estate, my property of any kind and nature, and anything I have an interest in (all of which is called the "residue"), so long as any such thing was not transferred by other Will provisions, as follows:

a) to _____Ruth May Kent my wife_____ who survive me with persons just named who survive me taking the share of non-survivors, then

b) to 45% to Oscar Elliot Kent my son and 45% to Karen Lisa Lundy my daughter and 10% to Pedro Juan Sanchez and if any of those just named do not survive me their part goes to their lineal descendants, per stirpes.

**4. ADMINISTRATION.** I name and appoint __Ruth May Kent__ as Executor including for me, my Will, and my estate.

**5. GUARDIAN.** I name __Karen Lisa Fox my sister__ as Guardian of the Person with control, authority, and custody of any minor child of mine, and also as Guardian of the Estate with control and authority over any minor child's property, money, and estate.

**6. MISCELLANEOUS.** The following applies to this Will and generally.

As Testator I agree and say I am a California resident and California should apply to this Will and all related issues and matters, and I request this be done.

Priority of Will gifts of the same type is based on the order they are written.

In this document no unfilled part is a mistake and residue spaces may be left blank.

The words "give" and "gift" also means a devise, bequest, grant, legacy, or similar.

A gift of property no longer owned by Testator at death shall lapse and be of no effect including no payment of money shall be done in its place, all without ademption.

If gift or gift section mentions survival, survive, or surviving then survival is an absolute condition and anti-lapse laws or similar have no effect.

Any failure to make gifts to family including children is intentional and not a mistake.

No gift or transfer made during life reduces or offsets a Will gift unless during my life I expressly usually called it a "loan" or "advancement".

Use of particular gender shall include other genders, reference to singular or plural shall include the other, and "they" may be singular or plural.

An Executor shall not have to give or file annual or other accountings about any money or property including in relation to my Will or estate, and they may act independently in all ways without supervision including through Independent Administration.

Executor is entitled to $900 as compensation for their work and nothing more and not as any fee schedule provides, and I do sincerely thank them for helping me and my estate. I suggest if a lawyer is needed one is hired who charges less than the standard fee schedule.

The residue includes lapsed or failed gifts, insurance paid to estate, inheritances owed me, and property I had a power of appointment or testamentary disposition over.

This Will does not revoke a Living Will or any legal document concerning health care.

Any Executor in their sole discretion may transfer money or property of any minor under age 18 at any time to a Custodian under the California Uniform Transfers To Minors Act or any similar law in any place. Custodian will manage, make discretionary payments of any kind and to any recipient to benefit the minor, and pay any remainder to the minor at age 18. I name as Custodian the Guardian of the Estate named in this Will, or if they fail to serve the Executor named in this Will. Executor also may select the Custodian. When doing this no bond, court action, or anything is required of Custodian or Executor.

## TESTATOR

IN WITNESS WHEREOF, I, __Paul Brian Kent__, the Testator, publish, declare, and sign this instrument as my Will this _30th_ day of __December__, 20 _19_, and do hereby declare that I signed this Will while both persons named as Witnesses were present after I asked them to witness my execution of my Will, that I am age 18 or older, that I am now of sound mind and memory, and that I do and execute this Will voluntarily for the purposes expressed in it and not due to duress, menace, fraud or undue influence.

*Paul Brian Kent*
Testator signature

## WITNESSES

On the date written below the Testator named above declared to us persons signing below as Witnesses that this instrument was the Testator's Will, and Testator asked us to witness it and act as Witnesses.

We the persons signing below understand that this instrument is the Testator's Will.

The Testator signed this Will when both of us persons signing below were present.

At the Testator's request, in the Testator's presence, and in the presence of one another, we sign our names as Witnesses.

We believe the Testator is age 18 or older, is of sound mind and memory, and to the best of our knowledge this Will was not procured by duress, menace, fraud or undue influence.

Each of us persons signing below is age 18 or older and is a competent witness.

We declare under penalty of perjury under California law the above is true and correct.

Executed on the _30th_ day of __December__, 20 _19_, at , __Venice__, California.

___Olivia Joy Pawlenty___          87 Shipwreck Road, Vacaville, CA  93704
Witness                                     Witness Address


___Roy Felix Pawlenty___          87 Shipwreck Road, Vacaville, CA  93704
Witness                                     Witness Address

# LAST WILL AND TESTAMENT

I, **David Eric Smith**, of **Fremont,** California, do revoke all prior Wills, Testaments, and Codicils, and do make, publish, and declare this as my Will. I am of sound mind and under no duress or undue influence and acting voluntarily.

**1. GIFTS.** I give these gifts in this Will, but to get a gift in this section the recipient must survive me except as otherwise stated below.

I give _____ $500 _____ to each of my brothers, sisters, and cousins _____ .

I give _____ $1000 _____ to Holy Spirit Food Shelf in Beverly Hills, California, 90210 .

**2. SEPARATE WRITINGS.** I may gift tangible personal property by writings separate from this Will as allowed by state law. Such a writing existing when this Will is done is not revoked or canceled unless this Will specifically says this. Such a writing not found within 90 days of my death is canceled and of no effect.

**3. RESIDUE.** The rest and residue and remainder of my estate, my property of any kind and nature, and anything I have an interest in, I give to **Adam Michael Smith and Ann Sue Baker who survive me** and to lineal descendants per stirpes of a person just named who did not survive me.

**4. ADMINISTRATION.** I name and appoint **Ann Sue Baker** as Executor including for me, my Will, and my estate.

**5. MISCELLANEOUS.** The following applies to this Will and generally.

As Testator I agree and say I am a California resident and California should apply to this Will and all related issues and matters, and I request this be done.

Priority of Will gifts of the same type is based on the order they are written.

In this document no unfilled part is a mistake and residue spaces may be left blank.

The words "give" and "gift" also means a devise, bequest, grant, legacy, or similar.

A gift of property no longer owned by Testator at death shall lapse and be of no effect including no payment of money shall be done in its place, all without ademption.

If gift or gift section mentions survival, survive, or surviving then survival is an absolute

condition and anti-lapse laws or similar have no effect.

Any failure to make gifts to family including children is intentional and not a mistake.

No gift or transfer made during life reduces or offsets a Will gift unless during my life I expressly usually called it a "loan" or "advancement".

Use of particular gender shall include other genders, reference to singular or plural shall include the other, and "they" may be singular or plural.

Unless parts of this Will specifically says otherwise a secured debt like mortgage or lien on real property or vehicles shall not be paid off, recipient of property takes it subject to liens, and no recipient who has debtor take property or get payment via use or threat of a secured debt may require a devisee, recipient, heir, or estate to pay or do anything.

I give any Executor a) the fullest authority, powers, and discretion allowed by state law, b) authority to lease, sell, mortgage, convey, or retain property including real property in any such manner and time they deem helpful or proper, c) authority to anytime settle or pay claims or debts if they in their sole discretion choose, and d) all other possible power.

An Executor shall not have to give or file annual or other accountings about any money or property including in relation to my Will or estate, and they may act independently in all ways without supervision including through Independent Administration.

Executor is entitled to $900 as compensation for their work and nothing more and not as any fee schedule provides, and I do sincerely thank them for helping me and my estate. I suggest if a lawyer is needed one is hired who charges less than the standard fee schedule.

I request informal or administrative probate of my Will and estate and summary action.

If context permits the terms Executor, Personal Representative, and Administrator shall be interchangeable as if all were written, and if context permits Guardian of any type shall be interchangeable with Conservator and Guardian of Property.

The residue includes lapsed or failed gifts, insurance paid to estate, inheritances owed me, and property I had a power of appointment or testamentary disposition over.

Any Executor, Guardian of any kind, Personal Representative, Conservator, Custodian, and any fiduciary under this Will or otherwise, shall qualify and serve without bond, security, surety, or similar, and despite their residence or lack of connections to a place.

This Will does not revoke a Living Will or any legal document concerning health care.

Any Executor in their sole discretion may transfer money or property of any minor under age 18 at any time to a Custodian under the California Uniform Transfers To Minors Act or any similar law in any place. Custodian will manage, make discretionary payments of any kind and to any recipient to benefit the minor, and pay any remainder to the minor at age 18. I name as Custodian the Guardian of the Estate named in this Will, or if they fail to serve the Executor named in this Will. Executor also may select the Custodian. When doing this no bond, court action, or anything is required of Custodian or Executor.

## TESTATOR

IN WITNESS WHEREOF, I, **David Eric Smith**, the Testator, publish, declare, and sign this instrument as my Will this **21st** day of **June**, 2021, and do hereby declare that I signed this Will while both persons named as Witnesses were present after I asked them to witness my execution of my Will, that I am age 18 or older, that I am now of sound mind and memory, and that I do and execute this Will voluntarily for the purposes expressed in it and not due to duress, menace, fraud or undue influence.

*David Eric Smith*
_____
Testator signature

## WITNESSES

On the date written below the Testator named above declared to us persons signing below as Witnesses that this instrument was the Testator's Will, and Testator asked us to witness it and act as Witnesses.

We the persons signing below understand that this instrument is the Testator's Will.

The Testator signed this Will when both of us persons signing below were present.

At the Testator's request, in the Testator's presence, and in the presence of one another, we sign our names as Witnesses.

We believe the Testator is age 18 or older, is of sound mind and memory, and to the best of our knowledge this Will was not procured by duress, menace, fraud or undue influence.

Each of us persons signing below is age 18 or older and is a competent witness.

We declare under penalty of perjury under California law the above is true and correct.

Executed on the **21st** day of **June**, 2021, at **Fremont**, California.

*Harriet Potter*
_____
Witness signature

204 Main Street, Fresno, CA  93650
_____
Witness address

*Pamela Bonnie Rooker*
_____
Witness signature

27 Woodbine Road, Fresno Heights, CA 93687
_____
Witness address

# TANGIBLE PERSONAL PROPERTY LIST

In this writing are gifts of tangible personal property to occur at my death, but this writing if not found by someone within 90 days of my death is void and canceled.

I may do many of these writings which should be seen as 1 document with the more recent writing controlling if any gifts conflict.

If a person getting a gift below does not survive me such gift is void and canceled.

| PROPERTY ITEMS | | NAMES OF RECIPIENTS |
|---|---|---|
| 1998 Ford Truck | to | Paul Rogers |
| 1.3 carat diamond ring + Irish rings | to | James Wong |
| 14 ft power boat + kayak + paddles | to | Larry Wheeler |
| Amish style bench | to | Rebecca Stewart |
| glass table, telescope, umbrellas | to | Kailani Stewart |
| Irish wood cups, oak platter, red vase | to | Mary and Cindy Lott |
| painting of sailboat in storm | to | Mary Lott |
| chainsaw marked with 382937 | to | Mary Lott |
| chainsaw marked with 89930 | to | Matt Smith |
| antique lanterns + repair kits | to | Sue Wu maid at Hart Hotel |
| oak lamp kept on porch | to | Mary Kay Poppler |
| sewing machines | to | Mary Kay Poppler |
| rocking chair bought in Oregon | to | Don Winkler boat mechanic |
| all fishing poles and fishing nets | to | Joe "Fish" Hoss, fishing pal |
| hats at cabin | to | Ken Baker |
| | to | |
| | to | |

DATE: _2-12-2023_     SIGNED: _David Eric Smith_